The *Glory* *of the* *Lamb*

Exploring the Depths
of God's Eternal Sacrifice

Sandy Davis Kirk, Ph.D.

McDougal Publishing is a ministry of The McDougal Foundation, Inc., a Maryland nonprofit corporation dedicated to spreading the Gospel of the Lord Jesus Christ to as many people as possible in the shortest time possible.

Published by:
McDougal Publishing
P.O. Box 3595
Hagerstown, MD 21742-3595
www.mcdougalpublishing.com

ISBN 978-1-58158-116-4

Printed in the United States of America
For Worldwide Distribution

Dedication

To my beloved students,
whose hearts have been "forever scarred"
by a revelation of the Lamb

Acknowledgments

When the Holy Spirit breathes a book, He raises up special people to encourage the author along the way. Above all, my students inspired me to believe that the time at last has come. When I saw how He seared the message of the Lamb into their hearts and took their passion even deeper, I knew a generation had arisen who would release *the Glory of the Lamb* to the world.

A constant source of blessing has been Pastors Chris and Susan Clay from England. Not only do the Clays preach the power of the Lamb in their church and on missionary journeys, but they watched their own daughter transformed by the power of the Lamb here at Brownsville. They have urged me not to back down in preaching the message of the cross and to always call a generation to behold the Lamb of God.

Also, our pastors at Brownsville, Pastors Randy and Suzann Feldschau, have carried our revival church and ministry school through a massive transition and prepared us for a fresh outpouring of *the Glory of the Lamb*. Their support of the message of the Lamb has inspired me deeply.

Finally, I must mention Mel Gibson's film, "The Passion of the Christ," which lifts the veil off the Lamb and shows the world His suffering. This book comes out shortly after the movie and will help to graphically explain the eternal significance of what that film courageously reveals on the screen.

For at last the time has come. Now the Father's heart will be satisfied as His Son receives the reward He deserves for giving His life as God's Lamb.

Contents

Introduction: **SCARRED HEARTS** 9

1. **Eternal Glory** 13
   The Lamb, Slain Before the World's Creation

2. **Creation's Glory** 25
   The Glory of the Son in the Garden of Eden

3. **Behold His Glory** 37
   Lambs Throughout the Bible

4. **Glory in Human Flesh** 49
   The Incarnation of Jesus Christ

5. **The Glory of the Cup** 61
   Why Did Jesus Sweat Blood in the Garden?

6. **The Glory of His Love** 75
   When the Son Drank His Father's Cup

7. **Resurrection Glory** 87
   The Resurrection and Ascension of the Lamb

8. **Exaltation Glory** 101
Unveiling the Eternal Glory of the Lamb

9. **The Glory He Deserves** 115
Glorifying the Son for Becoming the Lamb

"Then I saw a Lamb, looking as if it had been slain, standing in the center of the throne."

Revelation 5:6

"He is the sole expression of the glory of God [the Light-being, the out-raying or radiance of the divine]."

Hebrews 1:3, AMP

"The city does not need the sun or the moon to shine on it, for the glory of God gives it light, and the Lamb is its lamp."

Revelation 21:23

Introduction: Scarred Hearts

I broke into tears when I read David's note: "My heart will be forever scarred by a revelation of the Lamb!"

I wept, because nothing means more to me than seeing the Holy Spirit draw His sword through the soul of a young generation. Charles Spurgeon said, "We see the Lord pierced, and the piercing of our hearts begins."[1]

I saw this heart-piercing one Sunday afternoon at our camp as I read this book to a group of my Brownsville School of Revival students. They quietly wiped away tears, but when we came to the chapters on the Father's cup, something amazing happened.

They began to weep; some even wailed. It was as though an unseen hand had reached in and torn open their hearts. One student said, "When I looked at the Lamb and the cup that He drank, I felt a sword pierce my heart. A veil lifted and I could see Jesus as never before."

Then she said, insightfully, "Everyone hungers for more of God's glory, but we'll never see the glory until we've seen the Lamb!"

Could this be true?

Could the Holy Spirit be holding back the coming wave of glory until we are gripped with a passion for the Lamb, the One from whom the glory flows? Desperately we hunger for

God's glory, but could He hunger for something from us? Maybe the fountain won't fully open over us until we've gazed with trembling hearts upon the Fountainhead Himself.

Perhaps the final move of God will bring a revelation of the Lamb, even as the final book of the Bible brings a revelation of Jesus as the Lamb. Maybe God is waiting for our hearts to be scarred by the sacrifice of His Son as the Lamb.

Indeed, only a wounded God can heal the wounds of a bleeding world. Sadly, however, many people today are turned off by the hype and hypocrisy, the backbiting and bickering they've seen in churches. The world waits to see something real. When they hear the message of a crucified God, pouring from crucified hearts, then they will believe.

Frederick Faber wrote, "Only to sit and think of God — oh, what a joy it is! To think the thought, to breathe the name — earth has no higher bliss."[2] So I invite you now, through these pages, to simply gaze upon God. See *the Glory of the Lamb* before creation, all through the Old Testament, then robed in human flesh as He walks upon this earth.

Most of all, come stand on a little hill and gaze up at the Lamb of Glory, sagging from two planks of wood, streams of blood coursing down His cheeks, dripping from His chin and beard. Hear Him howl like a wounded animal as He drinks His Father's cup. Jonathan Edwards said that Jesus' "principal errand" for coming to earth was to drink this cup.[3] As you read about the Father's cup, let its contents burn deep, until your one consuming passion is to bring glory to the Son for giving His life as the Lamb.

Then watch the Lamb of God rise from the dead as resurrection power explodes from His heart, flooding the tomb with glory. See the Pierced One ascend into Heaven as His glory floods the timeless realms of Eternity, for *"He is the sole expression of the glory of God [the Light-being, the out-raying or radiance of the divine]"* (Heb. 1:3, AMP).

So come with me through the pages of this little book as we gaze deeply at the Lamb. We'll also go inside scenes of revival at our Bible college to see what is happening in the lives of many students. Here, in the midst of the revival of these young hearts, the Lord has been quietly doing something beautiful. I'm sure He wants to do this in your life, too.

Come now to an island near Greece in the midst of the Aegean Sea. Let's look through the window of the book of Revelation. Let's see through the eyes of the apostle John as he receives an unfolding revelation of the Lamb. Look deeply at the Wounded One upon the throne until your own heart is forever scarred by a revelation of *the Glory of the Lamb.*

Sandy Davis Kirk
Pensacola, Florida

Endnotes
1. Charles Spurgeon, "How Hearts Are Softened," *Spurgeon's Expository Encyclopedia,* Vol. 8 (Grand Rapids, MI: Baker Book House, 1977), p. 377.
2. Frederick W. Faber, cited in A.W. Tozer, *The Knowledge of the Holy* (San Francisco: Harper Collins Publishing, 1961), p. 12.
3. Jonathan Edwards, "Christ's Agony," *The Works of Jonathan Edwards,* Vol. 2 (Edinburgh: Banner of Truth Trust, 1995), p. 867.

One

Eternal Glory

The Lamb, Slain Before the World's Creation

John gazes out over the Aegean Sea, watching the sun cast an orange glow across the rippling waters. He closes his eyes to worship. Tears cling to his lashes as he pours out his love to his Lord.

Suddenly, he feels the Holy Spirit settle over him. His heart trembles and his whole being warms with the presence of God. He looks up and sees Heaven open. He gazes into the throne room and hears a voice cry, "Behold the Lion of the tribe of Judah!"

The old apostle squints the eyes of his spirit to look. What he sees takes his breath away.

There stands Jesus. He looks like *"a Lamb standing, as though it had been slain"* (Revelation 5:6, AMP).

The Lamb

John's heart fills with emotion, and tears burst from his eyes. "Oh, my Jesus!" he cries, scrambling to his feet. Though he is over ninety years old, the sight of his Lord causes strength to rush through his body. He reaches up with all his might as if to touch the feet of God.

John is amazed at the sight. This is the Man he walked with for over three years. He stood beside Him as He reached out and touched the oozing sores of lepers and the sightless eyes of beggars. He watched Him weep and pray and sweat blood in the garden.

He looked on as the whip ripped through His human flesh and the nails bored through His hands and feet. He gazed at the blood and tears dripping down His face and matting in crusty drops in His beard. He saw Him engulf every burning drop of the Father's cup. He beheld His side, streaming with blood and water.

He was there when Jesus walked through the walls in the Upper Room on Resurrection Day, showing those present the wounds still carved in His flesh. He stood on the Mount of Olives and saw Him as He ascended, caught away by a shining cloud. But now He sees Him standing in the throne room, still bearing wounds like a slain Lamb.

Here stands Jesus like a gleaming lamp, glory shining out from within Him and filling all of Heaven with His light. Thunder peals and lightning flashes from the throne. Rainbows of brilliance flood the eternal realm, but every eye focuses on One Person — God's Son who looks like a Lamb. *"He is the sole expression of the glory of God [the Light-being, the out-raying or radiance of the divine]"* (Hebrews 1:3, AMP).

John hears myriads of angelic beings, the seraphim, the

cherubim, the heavenly Sanhedrin, worshiping the Lamb. He crumples in a heap onto the rocks, for at last he knows, really knows — Jesus is receiving the glory He deserves for what He suffered as a Lamb.

Nothing means more to the old apostle. This was his highest passion. It was his driving motive and his purest ambition. Above all else, he wanted Jesus to receive the reward of His suffering. Just as the scripture says, *"He will see the result of the suffering of his soul and be satisfied"* (Isaiah 53:11, MT).[1]

John rubs his eyes and focuses on the Lamb. As he does, a revelation of the Lamb rushes over him. He swallows against the tightness in his throat, for he knows this glory traces back to *the Glory of the Lamb* before the world was ever made.

Slain Before Creation

For a moment the old apostle dares to imagine what took place in the Godhead, between Father, Son and Holy Spirit, before creation. In holy awe, the cheeks of his face glowing with the spirit of revelation, he thinks what it must have been like when God the Father turned to God the Son and asked, "Son, will You lay down Your life as a Lamb?"

All Heaven must have paused, paralyzed by such a profound question. Seraphim, if created yet, must have halted their antiphonal worship in mid-air. Cherubim must have buried their faces in their wings and wept. For there in the glory of Eternity, before worlds tumbled into space and stars dazzled the universe, the Father spoke. We don't have an exact account of the words, but perhaps it was something like this:

My Son, will You tear Yourself from My side and step down from the bliss of Eternity? Will You enter a fallen world of sin and death and pain?

Will You lay aside Your robes of glory, and robe Yourself in human flesh? Then will You allow Your body to be skinned and flayed in pieces, nails driven through hands and feet, back and chest ripped to bloody shreds, arms and legs wrenched in agony? And with Your human flesh torn and bleeding like a morning sacrifice, Your tongue swollen and stuck to the roof of Your mouth, will You allow Me to shove the filth of human sin upon You?

At this point, the Father must have paused to wipe away a tear. Then, with deep emotion, He continued:

My Beloved, will You hang in shame and pain as I withdraw My presence from You and You are utterly forsaken by Your Father God? Will You then open wide and drink down every drop of My cup of wrath? While bleeding from every wound, will You allow Me to plunge You into the punishment that humans deserve for sin? Will You do this all alone?

Will You then go into the dark grave until You arise, with beams of resurrection glory breaking out from Your heart? Then You will return to Your throne beside Me where You will be exalted *"to the highest place"* (Philippians 2:9). My Son, will You become the Lamb slain from the creation of the world? (See Revelation 13:8.)

Here from the island of Patmos, as John meditates on this amazing conversation, he realizes that this was actually the foundation of the Eternal Covenant of Redemption. In fact, Abraham's covenant and all other biblical covenants were based on this eternal covenant, transacted in the Triune Godhead in timeless, spaceless Eternity.[2]

Now the old apostle, still picturing in his mind this profound discussion between Father, Son and Holy Spirit, imagines God the Son slowly closing His eyes and bowing His head as He pondered this monumental request of the Father.

Surely silence filled the halls of Infinitude. No seraph in Eternity breathed a sound. Angels stood amazed.

Timeless moments passed as the Son looked ahead and saw what He would endure. He saw Himself on two stakes of wood, stripped of His robe of glory, robed instead in naked, bleeding flesh. He saw Himself crushed with sin and cast into the raging flames of wrath and punishment. But

He also saw resurrection power imploding His being and exploding from His heart. He saw Himself ascending to the throne and receiving a bride cleansed of sin and clothed in His glory.

What's more — He saw *you*.

And so, *"for the joy set before him"* (Hebrews 12:2), He lifted up His face and looked into His Father's eyes. With tears streaming from His eyes and love spilling from His heart, He cried with all His might: *"Yes, Father, I will go! I will offer Myself as a Lamb!"*

Angelic hosts must have fallen prostrate before God the Son, who agreed to offer Himself as a Lamb. They didn't fully understand this Everlasting Covenant of Redemption, for *"angels long to look into these things"* (1 Peter 1:12).

Heavenly beings could not imagine how One who was adored by angels could be *"despised and rejected by men"* (Isaiah 53:3). Creation had not yet occurred, so tissue bleeding, eyes weeping, whips slashing, thorns gouging, nails driving, spears thrusting would not register in their understanding.

How could uncreated Majesty stoop to such misery? How could One who has no beginning and no ending submit to death on a cross? How could the Crowned Prince become a crushed worm? How could the triumphant Lord become a tortured Lamb? They didn't know, so all they could do was fall on their faces and cry, *"Holy, holy, holy...."*

Then the Father must have lifted His mighty arm and

thundered through the halls of Eternity: *"Behold the Lamb, slain before the creation of the world!"* (See Revelation 13:8.)

All Heaven must have flooded with glorious praise. Seraphim — "the fiery ones" — flamed more brightly as they proclaimed His holiness. Cherubim wept in awe as they sang. Holy adoration flooded the limitless realms of Infinitude. Worship from the tongues of angels streamed through boundless, timeless Eternity.

The Sole Expression of Glory

We stand today on the earth, peeking through the window of scripture and looking through John's eyes at this divine celebration. And yet, if we could actually see what John saw, would the brightness blind our human eyes?

Paul was blind for three days after he saw the glory of Jesus. He tells us that Jesus dwells in *"unapproachable light, whom no one has seen or can see"* (1 Timothy 6:16). Moses glowed for months, although he had been shielded by a rock as God's glory trailed by him. The reason seraphim burned, Moses glowed and Paul was blind was because they had all been gazing on the glory of the eternal Lamb.

That's why the theme verse of this entire book is: *"He is the sole expression of the glory of God [the Light-being, the outraying or radiance of the divine]"* (Hebrews 1:3, AMP). In these pages we will dare to look through John's eyes to see this glory, shining from Eternity to Eternity. I pray that as you read, you will experience His presence flowing down upon you, warming your face and consuming your heart. I pray that you will breathe in the breath of God, and that you will feel the resurrection power of the Lamb coursing through your veins.

Carving a Vision

I have the privilege of teaching at the Brownsville Revival School of Ministry (BRSM) in Pensacola as well as leading a revival camp for the young generation. As I've poured my heart into young lives, I've been deeply struck by the pain throbbing in their hearts. All the divorces and absent fathers in our generation have left them numb. That's why so many have tried to dull the pain with drugs, drinking and sex.

But at BRSM, students are coming alive in the presence of God. As President Richard Crisco leads them in early morning prayer, Heaven opens and the Holy Spirit floods them. You can feel His presence in classes all through the day.

Lately, I've been weeping a lot as I've seen the Holy Spirit carve a vision of the Lamb into the hearts of students. It's a revelation that keeps them from sliding back into sin because it pierces their hearts. A pastor's wife told me, "My daughter has had many powerful experiences with God, but an hour on the floor, laughing in the presence of God, couldn't keep her from sin. What finally captured her heart and held her in holiness was when she saw the Lamb."

Victor was already a passionate revival student, but he told me, "When I saw the cup Jesus drank for me, it broke me. I cried and cried and cried. Through this brokenness, my passion burned deeper. Understanding what Jesus did for me anchored my heart forever."

One night I heard Ryan pacing through our camp, his face red with passion and his heart bursting with holy fire as he cried out to God: "Holy Spirit, for the rest of my life I will preach only Jesus Christ and Him crucified! May my heart be pierced every day by the Pierced One! May I always feel Your wound in my heart! Keep my feet walking in His bloody footsteps!"

This is why we need to come back to the Lamb. Even in the midst of glorious revival and powerful manifestations of the Holy Spirit, it's a revelation of the Lamb that will grip our hearts forever. Like the pastor's wife said about her daughter, it will hold our hearts in holiness when we see the Lamb.

The Forgotten Lamb

Often in times of revival or great outpourings of God's glory, we enjoy the feeling, but we fail to keep our focus on the One from whom the glory flows. In Heaven the Lamb of God is the central focus, the shining lamp, the sunlight of the city of God (see Revelation 21:23). We love the glory, but sometimes we don't look deep enough to see the One behind the glory.

That's why, in this book, we will focus on the Lamb of God, for He is the Fountainhead of God's glory. I pray that as you read, the eyes of your heart will begin to see God's humble, bleeding Lamb. I pray that He will be so vivid to you that you can almost reach up and touch the spikes in His hands and feet and almost run your fingers through the stripes in His flesh.

You see, something has been forgotten in the postmodern Church. In the midst of bustling programs, flourishing megachurches and personal ambition for success, we've sometimes overlooked the most important aspect of the Christian faith. We've forgotten God's Lamb.

It's like the story of the parents who held a christening party for their two-year-old boy. In the midst of the celebration the toddler wandered out the back door and slipped into the swimming pool. When he was found, it was too late. The next day, headlines read, "Baby Drowns at His Own Christening Party!"

That's what we've done in the Church. Once a year we may hear about the whip and thorns and nails, but when have we ever looked into the contents of the Father's cup? If this was the "principal errand" that the Son came to carry out on earth, as Jonathan Edwards said,[3] then why have we so neglected the subject? If this was the pinnacle of His sacrifice, why have we overlooked it for over 250 years in the Church? You see, in the middle of His own celebration, we've let the Baby drown.[4]

It's time to bring Him out of the shadowy deep and give Him the position He deserves. It's time to place the Lamb — who is the centerpiece of Heaven — as the centerpiece of the Church. It's time for the throne room scenes above to be revealed upon this earth. It's time for the Lamb to receive the glory on earth that He receives in Heaven.

Most of all, it's time for *you* to receive a revelation of the Lamb. He will become your highest passion, your purest motive, the driving purpose of your life.

Would you let Him begin right now? Simply open up your heart and come like a little child. Let His pure eyes search your soul and show you everything that keeps His presence away.

Look up to the Holy One — to the Lamb who still bears wounds in His flesh. See your sin in the bright light of His holiness. Tell Him you're sorry for all that's blocked your vision of Him, and let His blood wash you perfectly clean.

If you've never invited Him into your heart, call upon Him now. Ask Jesus to come and live inside you. Receive Him as your Savior and Lord.

Now ask the Holy Spirit to come. Speak to Him, the Spirit of Glory, and invite Him to come upon you and within you. Whisper, "Come, Holy Spirit. Come now...."

Wait until you feel Him flowing over you like a soft summer breeze. Open wide and breathe Him in. Let Him fill every pore of your being with His presence. Rest in His presence and don't come out until you feel Him lift.

Now let's return to the island to look through John's eyes at the wounded, bleeding, gleaming Lamb. From beginning to end, from alpha to omega, from Eternity to Eternity, come gaze upon Jesus, shining with *the Glory of the Lamb.*

Endnotes

1. From the Masoretic Text, which is the original Hebrew text.
2. This covenant is referred to in Isaiah 55:3, Ezekiel 37:26 and Hebrews 13:20. It is the covenant on which the Adamic, the Noahic, the Mosaic, the Davidic and the New Covenant in His blood all rest. This covenant in the Triune Godhead before the creation of the world is called "the Covenant of Redemption" (Wayne Grudem, *Systematic Theology,* Leicester, England: InterVarsity Press, 1994), pp. 518-519.
3. Jonathan Edwards, "Christ's Agony," *The Works of Jonathan Edwards*, Vol. 2 (Edinburgh: Banner of Truth Trust, 1995), p. 867.
4. While virtually all evangelical Bible colleges and seminaries teach on the penal substitution of Jesus, rarely is this preached in today's pulpits.

Two

Creation's Glory
The Glory of the Son in the Garden of Eden

The old apostle sits on the rocky ledge, gazing into Heaven. An iron ball hangs on a chain clamped to his ankle. He has been banished to this island for *"the word of God and the testimony of Jesus"* (Revelation 1:9). Yet he hardly notices his chains. Even as sunlight swallows up the light of the moon, the glory of God's presence swallows up the sorrow of his persecution.

John pulls out a scroll and begins writing. He knows the vision must be recorded so that others can receive this revelation. As he writes, he can feel his pulse racing and His face burning with the revelation of the Lamb.

Twenty-nine times he describes the Lamb of God in the book of Revelation. In fact, the word *revelation* in Greek is *apokalypsis*, which means, "an uncovering." Revelation comes from God, and in its truest sense means, "that which God uncovers about Himself." Our English word *revelation* comes from a Latin root which means, "to remove the veil."[1]

That's why John's revelation unveils *the Glory of the Lamb.*

Clothed in the Light of the Son

The warm flush of revelation burns on John's face as he thinks of the moment Elohim spoke at the dawn of creation. God said, *"Let there be light"* (Genesis 1:3), and suddenly the light of the Son burst out through the universe, flooding Infinitude with *the Glory of the Lamb.*

This was divine light, for sun, moon and stars would not be created until the fourth day (Genesis 1:14-15). It came, not from the light of the sun, but from the light of the Son.[2] On and on through timeless, spaceless Eternity flowed *the Glory of the Lamb,* for the Son is *"the sole expression of the glory of God [the Light-being, the out-raying or radiance of the divine]"* (Hebrews 1:3, AMP).

Now John thinks what it must have been like when *"God created the heavens and the earth"* (Genesis 1:1). John knows the Hebrew for *created* is *bārā,* which means, "to create out of absolutely nothing."

Then God the Son dipped into the clay of the earth to fashion the body of a man. *"For by him all things were created: things in heaven and on earth, visible and invisible, whether thrones or powers or rulers or authorities; all things were created by him and for him"* (Colossians 1:16).

John imagines the Son holding this corpse of clay to His breast, then breathing into his nostrils.

Suddenly, Adam inhales. Now his heart begins to beat,

and blood pulses through arteries and veins. Strength pours into muscles. Nerves begin to carry impulses to the brain. Vision fills his eyes as they flutter open.

Now Adam looks into the face of God. He gazes into the eyes of eternal love.

In that divine moment, God the Son smiles down on this son of His creation. Light from His face washes over Adam like an ocean wave, soaking him from head to foot, for the Son *"is the sole expression of the glory of God [the Light-being, the out-raying or radiance of the divine]"* (Hebrews 1:3, AMP).

Because sin has not yet entered his heart, Adam needs no protection from the glory. Moses would be hidden in the cleft of a rock, only seeing the back of God's trailing glory, but Adam walks in the unclouded glory of God. Naked and unashamed, he is clothed with *the Glory of the Lamb*.

Rûwach!

In Eden, the very air Adam breathes is filled with God's presence. It is God's breath, His *rûwach*, which is the Hebrew word meaning, "the breath or wind of God."

And now, as Adam walks with God in the "cool of the day," this means he walks in "the God-breathings of the day," for the word *cool* is this same Hebrew word *rûwach*.

John knows that *rûwach*, the breath of God, is used at least six times in Ezekiel 37. The Lord said, *"I will make breath [rûwach] enter you, and you will come to life"* (verse 5). *"Then he said to me, 'Prophesy to the breath' [rûwach]"* (verse 9). John knows by experience that the *rûwach* breathes life into dead bones.

He recalls the moment when God the Son breathed on him. Jesus had walked into the Upper Room after His resurrection. *"Receive the Holy Spirit"* (John 20:22), He said, breathing out over them all.

John inhaled, breathing in the breath of God like a fresh wind, causing his entire being to awaken. Before this, he had walked with Jesus and felt His divine presence, but now it was as though a holy wind came inside of him. He could feel the Holy Spirit filling his thirsty soul.

Even more wonderful, John remembers breathing in this *rûwach* of God on the day of Pentecost: *"Suddenly a sound like the blowing of a violent wind came from heaven and filled the whole house"* (Acts 2:2). John fell to his knees and breathed deeply of this divine wind of God. *I have never been the same since that day*, he thinks, tender emotion swelling in his heart.

God-Breathings of Revival

Robert Coleman, who is the director of the Institute of Evangelism at the Billy Graham Center at Wheaton College, defines revival as "breathing in the breath of God." He says, "Revival means, 'to wake up and live.'"[3]

When the breath of God swept into our church on Father's Day 1995, the church came alive with revival. For although darkness covers the earth and the nations shake with war and terror, God is breathing from Heaven and inviting us to breathe deeply of His glory-breath. He is at last awakening His Church and beginning to unveil to her a revelation of His glory.

You see, just five minutes in the presence and glory of God changes everything. I hear stories from students almost daily of how their lives were changed from being in this atmosphere. Many of them were full of drugs, hate and suicide, but when they visited the revival here at Brownsville, or any of the other wellheads of revival, their lives were completely changed. God's presence transforms, especially a starving young generation.

A Purpose Worth Dying For

When eighteen-year-old Mary arrived here from England, she was playful and rebellious and not the least bit interested in an encounter with God. She was simply here on a "holiday" to visit America. However, her wise parents, pastors of a church in Macclesfield, England, had offered to pay for the trip only if she stayed in Christian places.

After being here for two days, she encountered the presence of God and was overcome with conviction. Soon she was on her knees, weeping and crying out to God. She set aside all her plans to attend Nottingham University in England and came here to BRSM.

One Saturday night Mary accompanied me to a meeting with the evangelism students, where I had been invited to preach about the Lamb. During the message, I felt the Holy Spirit on me so strongly that I could barely talk, especially as I told about the Father's cup, which Jesus wept over in the garden and fully engulfed on the cross. (We'll see this in chapters five and six.)

After the message, I invited students to come forward so that I could pray for them to receive a revelation of the Lamb. I cannot impart this revelation to anyone, but I can pray and ask the Holy Spirit to do so. I started to pray, and then I saw Mary.

No one had touched her but she was on the floor, weeping her heart out. She had been saved for two months, but she later told me, "I *fell in love* with Jesus when I saw Him as the Lamb." The changes I saw in her after that were amazing.

When Mary returned to England for Christmas, she stood in her father's church and sincerely repented. She asked forgiveness for the double life she had led and told how she had found Jesus as the Lamb. She repented to her own father in front of everyone, and most of the people dissolved in tears. Repentance swept through the church and her father couldn't even preach. It was the early seeds of revival in a wonderful English church.

While she was home, one of her friends said, "Oh, so now you're not going with us to the pubs to drink and do all the things we used to do?" Mary looked at her with tears of love in her eyes. "Anna, God is *real*. He's *really real!*" she cried. One year later, Anna came here to visit and soon she was weeping out her sin at the feet of Jesus Christ.

After all, isn't that what this young generation is looking for? The hype they've seen in some Christian circles repulses them. The deadness they've seen in many churches leaves them cold. Skepticism and distrust riddle their thinking.

But when they see something *real*, when they feel the authentic presence of God flowing down upon them, they run to the river of God. Tears of love burst from their eyes and passion burns from their hearts, for they are desperately hungry for a tangible experience with God.

And when the Holy Spirit opens their hearts, drawing out the pain and filling them with a revelation of *the Glory of the Lamb*, they are forever changed. All they ever needed was a purpose worth dying for, so they could really live.

He Took the Fall

In the past few years, one of the anointed worship songs that opens Heaven and helps us see the Lamb is "Above All." The words of the chorus speak volumes to our hearts:

> *Crucified, laid behind a stone;*
> *You lived to die, rejected and alone.*
> *Like a rose, trampled on the ground,*
> *You took the Fall and thought of me,*
> *Above all.*[4]

Do you know what this means? Do you know how Jesus "took the Fall" of the human race on Himself?

First peek back into the Garden of Eden and see Adam and his wife, not called Eve until after the Fall (Genesis 3:20). See them bathed in the glory of God; now look up to the cross and see God the Son, laying aside His glory and bathing Himself in His own blood.

Look back and watch Adam walking in the sweet breathings of the presence of God in the cool of the day; now look up and watch God rip away His presence and blaze His wrath upon the Son in the heat of the day.

Glance back and see Adam and his wife lifting themselves up to become *"like God"* (Genesis 3:5); now look up to the Son lowering Himself to become "like a Lamb."

Look back and see a son hide from a Father behind a tree; now look up and see a Father hide from a Son, who hangs upon a tree.

Gaze back and hear God calling, "Son, where are you?" Now turn your gaze up to the cross and hear a Son calling, "My God, where are You?"

See Adam cast out of the garden to toil by the sweat of his brow; but look up and see Jesus toiling in prayer until the sweat of His brow turns to blood.

Look back and see God cursing the ground with piercing thistles and thorns; now look forward and see those thorns piercing the head of the Son.

You see, He "took the Fall" in every way, for at the Fall, a serpent was told he would bruise the heel of the Seed of the woman; now look up at the cross and see the Seed of the woman crush the serpent's head (see Genesis 3:15, NKJ; Colossians 2:15).[5]

Look back and see cherubim with flaming sword, guarding the way to the tree of life and the river of God. But look up to the Lamb and see a soldier's spear pierce the Tree of Life Himself, releasing the river of God.

Gaze back to the Fall and see Adam still bearing a scar where a bride was taken from his side. Now look up to the Lamb who still bears the scar where a Bride was taken from His side.

Look back to the Fall and see a son and daughter clothed with animal skins, probably lambs'; now look up to the One who clothes you with *the Glory of the Lamb*.

Yes, in every way, Jesus, the Lamb of God, took the Fall of the human race. In the words of the song: "Like a rose, trampled on the ground, You took the Fall and thought of me, above all."

He Thought of You

At the dawn of creation, Adam opened his eyes and looked into the face of God the Son. Won't you do the same?

Look up and open the eyes of your heart to the Son. See the glory-light beaming in His eyes. Feel the warmth of His smile, shining down upon you.

This is what He died to give you. Remember the words: "You took the Fall and thought of *me*, above all." Let that thought soak in deep. He thought of *you*. Say it to yourself: "He thought of *me*." Look into a mirror and say it into your own eyes: "He took the Fall and thought of *me*, above all!"

Believe it. Receive it.

Now, like Adam at creation, let His glory cover you. Let the One who is *"the sole expression of the glory of God"* clothe you. Let the *"Light-being, the out-raying or radiance of the divine,"* cloak you with creation's glory.

With the eyes of your heart, look into the face of the Son *"For God, who said, 'Let light shine out of darkness,' made his light shine in our hearts to give us the light of the knowledge of the glory of God in the face of Christ"* (2 Corinthians 4:6).

Drink in His presence until your face shines and your eyes blaze with the light of *the Glory of the Lamb*.

Endnotes

1. J. Rodman Williams, *Renewal Theology*, Vol. 1 (Grand Rapids, MI: Zondervan Publishing House, 1992), pp. 32-33.

2. J. Rodman Williams, *Renewal Theology*, Vol. 1, p. 110. Williams describes this "cosmic light" as "consisting of ether waves produced by energetic electrons. Another way of putting it is to think in terms of electromagnetic forces that were activated by the Word, thus calling light out of darkness." Williams quotes Carl F. H. Henry: "The light that shattered darkness on the first day of creation was not light emitted by heavenly luminaries (these were created on the fourth day, 1:14-19); it was rather the light mandated by Elohim to negate the darkness of chaos" (Carl F. H. Henry, in *God, Revelation and Authority*, Vol. 6, pt. 2 [Waco, TX: Word Publishers, 1976], p. 136).

3. Robert E. Coleman, "What Is Revival?" *Accounts of a Campus Revival*, Timothy K. Beougher and Lyle W. Dorsett, eds. (Wheaton, IL: Harold Shaw Publishers, 1995), pp. 13-14.

4. Paul Baloche and Lenny LeBlanc, "Above All" (Integrity's Hosanna Music/ASCAP & LenSongs Publishing, 1999).

5. Genesis 3:15 is called the Protevangelium, the first proclamation of the Gospel in the Old Testament.

Three

Behold His Glory
Lambs Throughout the Bible

John looks again at Jesus, and his whole being fills with awe. Nothing can rival this encounter with God. Brightness floods the atmosphere. Rainbows of splendor surround the throne. Jesus looks like a fountain of glory.

The presence of Christ pours down upon John. It is life and refreshing, power and joy. The old apostle drinks and drinks and drinks of this sweetness. As he does, he thinks about the sheer wonder of this glory that flows from the Lamb of God.

The Glory

John knows that the Hebrew word for "glory" is *kabôd*, meaning, "heavy, weighty, profoundly significant." Because His glory has weight, it can be experienced by the human senses.

In our day, J. Rodman Williams, in *Renewal Theology*, said that glory is the "splendor and majesty that shines through in every aspect of God's being and action."[1] Jonathan Edwards described glory as "the refulgence of God," shining down from Him and reflecting back to Him.[2] Francis Frangipane, in an interview on Christian television, simply called the glory "the nectar of God."[3]

But above all, the glory is the very essence that flows from the Lamb Himself. Jesus is the source, the container, the reservoir of the eternal glory of God.

John wipes the moisture on his face and closes his eyes, his tender heart yearning for the Lord. Simply to meditate on the glory overwhelms him, yet it deeply satisfies the aching hunger within him.

Lambs in the Old Testament

Now the old apostle's thoughts rush back to the slaying of lambs in the Hebrew Scriptures. He recalls Abel's sacrifice, accepted by God because blood flowed out from an innocent lamb (see Genesis 4:2-4). John knows this spoke of the blood of Jesus, the pure and innocent Lamb of God.

He remembers the Passover lamb, which God told Moses could never be eaten *raw or cooked in water, but roasted over the fire* (see Exodus 12:9-10). John knows these flames spoke of God's wrath and punishment, roasting the Lamb of God while He was suffering on the cross.

John thinks now about the sin offering on the Day of Atonement, or Yom Kippur, when the high priest sprinkled the blood seven times in front of the veil (see Leviticus

4:6,17). *Why seven?* John always wondered. Now in the bright light of revelation, John realizes that Jesus' flesh, which was the veil, was sprinkled seven times with His own blood.

The first was in Gethsemane when blood coated His brow and splotched His garments. The second was at the Roman Pavement when whips slashed His flesh. The third was when thorns punctured His brow. The fourth was when spikes were driven through His hands. The fifth was when spikes penetrated His feet. The sixth was when the spear pierced His side. The seventh came when Jesus' own heart ruptured and spilled out blood.[4]

This leads the apostle to think of the lambs for the daily burnt offering. John knows that when Aaron laid the whole burnt offering on the altar at the dedication of the Tabernacle, fire from heaven came down: *"Fire came out from the presence of the LORD and consumed the burnt offering and the fat portions on the altar"* (Leviticus 9:24).

John further remembers that when David called on the Lord and offered burnt offerings and fellowship offerings at the place where the Temple would be built, *"the LORD answered him with fire from heaven on the altar of burnt offering"* (1 Chronicles 21:26). Then when Solomon laid the burnt offering on the altar at the dedication of the Temple, *"fire came down from heaven and consumed the burnt offering and the sacrifices"* (2 Chronicles 7:1).

Why did fire from Heaven come down on all three of these sacrifices, as well as on Elijah's burnt offering on Mount

Carmel? (See 1 Kings 18:38.) It was because God was showing them that the fires of His eternal wrath — far worse than any literal, physical fire — would ultimately burn down on His own Son when He offered Himself as a burnt offering on the cross.

"Behold the Lamb of God!"

Now a lump fills John's throat as he remembers the day he stood beside the banks of a river and, for the first time, beheld the Lamb of God.

The waters of the Jordan River ran cold this time of year. Melting snows from Mount Hermon formed the headwaters of the Jordan, flowing down to the Sea of Galilee, then south to Jericho, emptying into the Dead Sea.

John stood amidst the throng that had gathered to be baptized by John the Baptist. The young disciple saw the rugged prophet look up suddenly from his baptizing.

The look on the Baptist's face betrayed his heart. It was as though a million suns had burst across his vision. His face flushed and his body shook.

Thirty years before, while he was in his mother's womb, his pregnant relative, Mary, had come into the courtyard to greet his mother, Elizabeth. Instantly, the Holy Spirit filled Elizabeth and John leapt inside his mother's womb.

Now, as the Baptist looked up and saw Jesus coming toward him, his spirit leapt again. He lifted his arm, trembling. Pointing toward Jesus, he thundered: *"Behold the Lamb of God, which taketh away the sin of the world!"* (John 1:29, KJV).

Now, with this brief sermon, probably the greatest sermon ever preached, the meaning of the lambs is explained. Jesus is the fulfillment of the Passover lambs, the fulfillment of the lambs for the daily burnt offering, and the fulfillment of the lamb for the sin offerings, whose blood ran like rivers in front of the great altar.

John's whole life forever changed the day he looked up and saw the Lamb of God. Your life, too, will be changed by beholding the Lamb. Spurgeon said, "To meditate much on the Lamb of God is to occupy your mind with the grandest subject of thought in the universe."[5]

The Crushed Lamb

Suddenly, the apostle's heart jolts as he looks back up to the Lamb. As he gazes on the marks, vividly etched into His flesh, his thoughts slip back to that moment when He looked up at Jesus on the cross.

He saw the tears etching down His cheeks, mixing with the spittle of snarling priests and soldiers. He saw the nails quivering in His hands and the fingers drawn up in a claw, as though He was grasping for God His Father. He saw the pain in His eyes and heard the agony in His cries.

Tears squeeze from John's eyes and a sob fills his throat as he thinks of the One who laid aside His robe of infinite glory to robe Himself in bloody shreds of flesh — eternal, yet dying as a man; omnipresent, yet stapled in one place on a cross; omnipotent, yet hanging powerless; omniscient, yet asking, *"My God, why?"*

The humility of God staggers John's senses. To think — the Highest stoops to become the lowest! The Greatest becomes the least! The King becomes a criminal! The Creator becomes the crucified! The Powerful One becomes the Pierced One!

John doubles over, weeping. He can hardly contain the emotion he feels, for he knows that when wrath broke over Jesus, He released from His eternal being floods of mercy, and grace, and love, and holiness, and all the numberless moral attributes of God. Then when He rose from the dead and poured down His Spirit at Pentecost, these attributes of God were released and flowed down like a mighty river.

Yes, the grape containing the sweet wine of glory was crushed to bleed out its goodness on us. Now we can partake of the nectar of God, the very nature of the Lamb.

One day in my Systematic Theology class, I tried to demonstrate this crushing. I poured water into a glass vase and asked the students to see this vase as the body of Jesus, filled with God's attributes of mercy and love and all of His moral attributes.[6] Then I took a hammer and began to beat the vase. "They beat Him with whips, pierced Him with thorns, and impaled Him with nails," I said. Then I raised the hammer and cried, "But when the Father's eternal wrath roared down upon Him, His heart burst open in a rupture." I smashed the bottom of the vase until it burst open, spilling the water into a plastic tub at my feet.

I reached down and picked up the vase, broken open at the bottom. Holding up what was left of this shattered vase, I said, "Now here was Jesus—an empty corpse—laid inside a tomb." I took a pitcher of water and poured it through the vase, saying, "But when the presence of the Holy Spirit invaded that tomb and flowed through this shell of His body, the power of God poured out from His being and flooded the tomb with resurrection glory! Now the attributes of God can flow down on you!"

I reached down and dipped a glass into the water in the tub. Pointing to the glass, I said, "Now here you are, filled with His goodness, and because Jesus poured out this river of life, you can now give cups of living water to other thirsty souls!"

The students were deeply touched as they received a visual image of what Jesus did for them as the Lamb. All we could do was worship.

Worshiping the Lamb

I saw this passion for the Lamb bursting from Lindell Cooley's heart, while he was still our worship leader at Brownsville. It was the first Friday night revival service of 2003, and with tears trembling in his voice, he paused in the midst of worship. He cried, "I'm so jealous for the Lord! I know many of you think this is just about music. I don't care about this music!" he cried. "I care about the heart of the One who died for me! I care about Him knowing how I feel about Him!"

He continued with passion, "When we get to this chorus, 'Worthy Is the Lamb,'...I wonder if all the passion in your heart could just explode up in your mouth, and you could turn it loose for the Lord."

Then he said, "The Bible in Revelation says, *'Worthy is the Lamb! Worthy is the Lamb who was slain!'* But we humans have no idea what that means. We think we do because we preach a good Easter sermon."

Then Lindell cried, "We have no idea that the Darling of Heaven, Jesus Christ, left a palace and came into a manger to die with criminals so that you and I don't have to die a spiritual death!"

With emotion swelling in his words, he shouted, "I who was a pauper! I who was a stealer and a thief and a liar! I who was ashamed! I who was held in addictions! In filth! I am now a child of God! 'Worthy! Worthy! Worthy,'" he shouted, then burst again into the song, "Worthy is the Lamb, seated on the throne!" The church exploded:

> *Crown Him now with many crowns*
> *Who reigns victorious,*
> *High and lifted up, Jesus Son of God;*
> *The Darling of Heaven crucified.*
> *Worthy is the Lamb!* [7]

On and on we worshiped the glorious Lamb of God, and as we did, it was as though a fountain of glory opened up over us. The presence of God electrified the atmosphere. Every breath we took was filled with holiness. Life from Heaven filled every crevice of our beings.

Indeed, it was joy indescribable, peace ineffable, power immeasurable, glory unfathomable. Nothing compared to the wonder of standing in the manifest presence of God. "The knowledge that God is present is blessed," wrote Tozer, "but to feel His presence is nothing less than sheer happiness."[8] Tears splashed down our faces as we lost ourselves in endless worship to the Lamb.

The Light of His Face

One day someone asked blind Fanny Crosby, author of thousands of Christians hymns, "Do you wish you had not been blinded?" She replied with a smile, "Well, the good thing about being blind is that the very first face I'll see will be the face of Jesus."[9]

I believe, however, that the reason Fanny Crosby could write such Christ-adoring hymns was because she had already seen the face of Jesus. With the eyes of her heart she had beheld the Lamb.

I believe the Holy Spirit wants to give you this vision too. He wants you to look into Eternity, like John, where you will behold God's eternal Lamb.

Why not do so even now? Close your physical eyes but stretch the eyes of your heart and reach your gaze into Heaven. Look through John's eyes at the only One in the Godhead whom he can actually see. He cannot see the Father, nor can he see the Holy Spirit, but he can see Jesus. You, too, can behold the God-Man, the One who looks like a slaughtered Lamb.

When you see Him, look into the face that shines as bright as the sun. See the love in His eyes. Feel the warmth of His smile. Drink deeply of His mercy, His grace, His love and His holiness. Saturate yourself in this fountain of light, as the psalmist wrote, *"You cause them to drink of the stream of Your pleasures. For with You is the fountain of life; in Your light, we see light"* (Psalm 36:8-9, AMP). Let the light of His face soak you through and through.

When my first grandbaby was born, his skin turned yellow from jaundice. The doctor told my daughter and me to place him in front of a window, with nothing clothing him but a diaper. Then, as he soaked up the rays of the sun, his bloodstream would be cleansed and soon his skin would be rosy and normal.

Most of us are like my grandbaby; our bloodstream is impure. We need to sit beneath the rays of God the Son and soak in the light of His glory.

If you'll do this daily, without even realizing it, as you behold the glory in the face of the Lamb, your bloodstream will purify and your face will begin to shine. You will be transformed as you reflect His glory: *"And we, who with unveiled faces all reflect the Lord's glory, are being transformed into his likeness with ever-increasing glory"* (2 Corinthians 3:18).

You see, just five minutes of gazing on the Lamb and soaking in His presence can change everything. It will soften your heart, refresh your soul, heal your emotions and give you an eternal perspective. Do this every day and you will be transformed by beholding *the Glory of the Lamb*.

Endnotes

1. J. Rodman Williams, *Renewal Theology,* Vol. 1 (Grand Rapids, MI: Zondervan, 1992) p. 79.
2. Jonathan Edwards, "God's Chief End in Creation," *The Works of Jonathan Edwards,* Vol. 1 (Edinburgh: Banner of Truth Trust, 1995), p. 119.
3. Francis Frangipane, on "Praise the Lord," Trinity Broadcasting Network, 2002.
4. See chapter six for more on the tearing of the veil of Jesus' flesh.
5. Charles Spurgeon, "Behold the Lamb," *Spurgeon's Expository Encyclopedia,* Vol. 3 (Grand Rapids, MI: Baker Book House, 1977), p. 110.
6. The moral attributes are His goodness, love, mercy, humility and all the numberless attributes which can be given to humans. His incommunicable, transcendent attributes are His omnipotence, omniscience, omnipresence, self-existence, eternality, immutability and all those attributes that cannot be given to humans.
7. Darlene Zschech, "Worthy Is the Lamb," from *You Are My World* (Hillsong Publishing, 2000).
8. Allen Fleece, cited in A. W. Tozer, *The Knowledge of the Holy,* (San Francisco: Harper Collins Publishing, 1961) p. 76.
9. Matt Redman, "The Unquenchable Worshiper," *Good News Magazine,* Vol 35, No. 6 (May/June 2002), p. 17.

Four

Glory in Human Flesh
The Incarnation of Jesus Christ

Ocean spray splashes the old apostle's face, mixing with tears and dribbling off his chin, but he is unaware. It seems the more he looks at the Lamb, the more light for revelation he receives. Like a morning sunrise bursting over earth's horizon, the light of revelation shines into his thirsty soul.

Now as John feels the unveiled glory streaming down from the Lamb of God in Heaven, he recalls what happened to the glory in the Old Testament.

Glory in the Holy of Holies

He recalls how the glory, cloaked in a cloud, hovered in the Holy of Holies of Moses' Tabernacle. Later it settled in David's Tabernacle, a little tent on Mount Zion in Jerusalem. Then, finally, the grand Temple of Solomon in Jerusalem became the resting place of God's glory.[1]

John knows, however, that the Babylonian army swept into Jerusalem and destroyed the beautiful Temple in 586 B.C. Ezekiel had a vision in which he saw the glory of the

Lord lifting off the Temple before it was destroyed. He saw the glory, resting on the wings of cherubim, hesitating over the threshold, as though it regretted leaving, then ascending over the mountain east of the city, which is the Mount of Olives (see Ezekiel 10:18-19; 11:23).

The glory was not seen again on earth for over four hundred years. Zerubbabel's Temple, sometimes called the Second Temple, was built, but elderly people wept aloud, for they knew the glory of God was missing (see Ezra 3:12).[2] And in New Testament days, Herod's Temple would be built, but still no glory would rest beyond the veil.

The glory would not return to earth until one quiet evening in the little town of Nazareth. Now, with a rush of joy sweeping over him, the old apostle thinks of the moment the glory came down, enfleshed in human skin.

The Incarnation

John closes his eyes. Tears hang on his lashes as he remembers hearing Mary tell the story. Reverently she told him what the angel Gabriel said to her: *"The Holy Spirit will come upon you, and the power of the Most High will overshadow you. So the holy one to be born will be called the Son of God"* (Luke 1:35). John knows that the Greek for *overshadow* is *episkiazō,* meaning, "to envelop in a haze of brilliancy."

John's mind is dazzled with the wonder of the Incarnation, which means God "in flesh." To think — He who sprinkled the universe with galaxies, stars and planets, making them out of absolutely nothing, was born in human flesh. He who made man was made a Man. He who cradled His head upon His Father's breast, now cradled His head in an animal feed trough. He whose glory filled Eternity, now filled a baby's body.

Spurgeon marveled:

> The infinite God who filleth all things, who was and is, and is to come, the Almighty, the Omniscient, and the Omnipresent, actually condescended to veil himself in the garments of our inferior clay. He made all things, and yet he deigned to take the flesh of a creature....The Infinite was linked with the infant, and the Eternal was blended with mortality.[3]

Theologians today call this the *hypostatic union*, the union of God and man, the merging of the divine with human nature.[4]

And yet He, *"being in very nature God, did not consider equality with God something to be grasped, but made himself nothing"* (Philippians 2:6-7). This self-emptying of the Son of God is called the *kenosis*, meaning, He gave up the independent exercise of His transcendent attributes and was completely dependent on the Father and the Holy Spirit.[5]

Flashes of His Glory

The old apostle thinks now of the gleams of glory he saw breaking all around the Lord. He remembers Mary telling of how the skies had burst with light and how angels had sung of His glory at His birth. When she and Joseph had brought Him to the Temple, the old prophet Simeon had rushed up, lifted Him in his arms and cried, "He is *a light for revelation to the Gentiles, and a glory for your people Israel!*" (see Luke 2:32). (In fact, John wrote so much about the glory of Jesus in his gospel that today his book is called "the gospel of the glory.")

Everywhere Jesus walked, John recalls, the place was aglow with God. He saw flashes of His glory shooting forth through His teachings and His miracles. That's why, in His first miracle at Cana, when He turned water into wine, John wrote, *"He thus revealed his glory"* (John 2:11). And just before raising Lazarus from the dead, Jesus said to Martha, *"Did I not tell you that if you believed, you would see the glory of God?"* (John 11:40).

But even more than the glory of His teachings and miracles, the glory of His compassion warmed John's heart. Sometimes, when he laid his own head upon the Master's chest, he could almost feel compassion surging in Jesus' breast.

The young disciple often saw the Lord looking out over the crowds with aching compassion (see Matthew 9:36, 14:14, 20:34). The Greek for *compassion* is *splanchnizomai*, meaning, "bowels that yearn with compassion." Though He came from Heaven where no tears or pain existed, He came to us in human flesh so He could know the sensation of hunger gnawing, tears falling, thirst burning, muscles aching, blood draining, pain wrenching.

Though He was fully God, Jesus knew the feeling of tears welling up in His eyes and swimming down His face. His tears were like liquid mercy, distilled in drops of moisture. They contained the passion and pathos of God, dissolved in fluid, dripping from His eyes. His tears showed the glory of His love, running down His face.[6]

Yet never did John see glory shining so brightly from Jesus' face as the night the young disciple followed Him up a high mountain to pray.

The Glory of Christ

It was almost midnight as they climbed. Patches of snow dotted the mountainside, reflecting the light of the moon. Finally, Jesus stopped, lifted His head in prayer, and began to shine.

John rubbed his eyes.

Jesus glowed as bright as the sunlight. The young disciple was awestruck. He could feel the light flooding out from Jesus. His heart drummed wildly in his chest and his own face glowed with the heat of the glory. So thick was God's presence that he could hardly breathe. It was like Heaven on earth.

It was as though the glory, which once shimmered behind the veil and rested over the ark, could no longer be contained by the veil of Jesus' flesh. Now the glory within

Him exuded out of every pore of His human skin. Charles Spurgeon said, "As the light streams through the lantern, so the glory of the Godhead streamed through the flesh of Jesus."[7]

That was the moment all doubts dissolved from young John. He had heard Jesus teach, had watched Him walk on water, had seen Him heal blind eyes and raise the dead. But as he beheld His glory there on the mountain, he knew that Jesus Christ was *God*. Thus he wrote, surely with trembling heart and shaking hand, *"We have seen his glory, the glory of the One and Only"* (John 1:14).

John knows, however, that he can never fully uncover the riches of the glory of Christ. Spurgeon said, "Even eternity will not be too long for the discovery of all the glory of God which shines forth in the person of the Word made flesh."[8]

In fact, the Bible says that the moon and sun will be ashamed in comparison with the glory of the Son: *"Then the moon will be confounded and the sun ashamed, when [they compare their ineffectual fire to the light of] the Lord of hosts"* (Isaiah 24:23, AMP).

You could step outside and look up at the sun in the sky until your eyes burn blind. But lift your eyes to the shining face of the Lamb, and your eyesight will purify, your gaze will grow stronger, your vision will clear, and your heart will burn with His glory.

Like Stephen who saw the face of Jesus, your own face will shine with the glory of God. Charles Spurgeon said of

Jesus, "He is the sun of our day; He is the star of our night; He is our life; He is our life's life; He is our heaven on earth, and He shall be our heaven in Heaven."[9] He is indeed *"the sole expression of the glory of God [the Light-being, the out-raying or radiance of the divine]"* (Hebrews 1:3, AMP).

A Sword Through the Soul

However, before we can really see the Lamb, something needs to happen in the depths of the human soul. It's like the time Simeon lifted up Baby Jesus in the Temple. He spoke of His glory, but his last words, though usually overlooked, are crucial to the Church today. He looked Mary straight in the eye and said, *"And a sword will pierce your own soul"* (Luke 2:35).

This is what needs to happen in the Church today. We need a piercing of our souls. It comes when our hearts are broken by His brokenness on the cross. Spurgeon said, "We see the Lord pierced, and the piercing of our hearts begins."[10]

That's why I broke into tears the day I walked into my office and saw a rose in a vase. In the attached note, David, one of my students, had written, *"My heart will be forever scarred by a revelation of the Lamb!"* I wept, because nothing means more to me than seeing the Holy Spirit pierce the hearts of a young generation.

Since then, students have continuously told me how the Holy Spirit has branded their hearts. At our BRSM graduation, Elizabeth testified, "Jesus has pierced my heart with a revelation of the Lamb!"

Could this be what Paul meant when he said, *"Circumcision is circumcision of the heart, by the Spirit"* (Romans 2:29)?

Indeed, when the Holy Spirit draws His sword through one's soul, it creates deep holiness of heart. One morning Leah came to me with tears of conviction in her eyes. She told me how the Lord had been pouring a revelation of the Lamb into her heart all summer. But in the light of His holiness, she had seen her own unholiness. Her voice shook as she looked me in the eyes and said, "I lied on two of your final exams."

With godly sorrow pouring from her heart, she admitted she had not completed all of her required reading, though she told me on the exam that she had. *I'll finish it this summer,* she had said to herself. *The Lord understands.* Now, in the bright light of the holiness of the Lamb, she was broken by her sin. We prayed together and she repented to the Lord. She finished her reading and her conscience cleared, but it all began with a heart-piercing revelation of the Lamb.

It was just like the pastor's wife had said about her daughter, "What captured her heart and held her in holiness was when she saw the Lamb."

My prayer is that the Holy Spirit will bring this revelation to His entire Church. But before we can really see through the scales of religion and materialism and vainglory in the Church today, we need the sword of the Lord to cut through the layers that cover our eyes.

It's like the story of the girl who had been blind since birth. She had never seen a sunset splash a western sky or watched a bird build a nest on a leafy branch. Most of all, she had never seen her father, who now stood anxiously by her bedside as a doctor loosened the bandages from an operation on her eyes.

Anticipation mounted within her as she thought, *Soon I'll see my daddy's face!* Finally, the last bandage was lifted and light struck her eyes. She blinked and slowly focused. She looked up and saw her father smiling down upon her. She tried to speak, but the words stuck in her throat. She reached up and touched his features. Then, finally, she burst out, "Oh, Daddy, you're more beautiful than I ever dreamed!"

So is Jesus. He's lovelier than we've ever dreamed, but we've all been somewhat blind. We've needed an operation on the eyes of our hearts so we can really see the Lamb.

So come now through the next two vital chapters, which are the heart of this book. Ask the Holy Spirit to draw His sword through your heart, giving you a divine revelation of the Lamb.

Pray that He will open to you the mystery and the glory of the cup, which Jesus drank for you on the cross. Ask Him to strike your heart with the full weight of this cup and then chisel a revelation of the Lamb into your very soul.

Come now with humility and hunger, for nothing so softens the heart as a long, steady look at the Lamb. Continuous looks produce continuous piercings, until calluses soften, scales tear away, numbness melts, and we can really see the magnitude of His sacrifice. Then, and only then, will we fully behold *the Glory of the Lamb.*

Endnotes

1. Solomon's Temple was described as having windows which were "narrow within but wide without." The rabbis said this was to keep the darkness of the world out of the sanctuary, but "to let the light of the Shekinah illumine the world." (Num. Rabbah 15.2, cited in D. Moody, "Shekinah," *The Interpreter's Dictionary of the Bible* [Nashville: Abingdon Press, 1962], p. 318).
2. Zerubbabel's Temple was completed in 516 B.C.
3. Charles Spurgeon, "The Great Mystery of Godliness," *Spurgeon's Expository Sermons*, Vol. 3 (Grand Rapids, MI: Baker Book House, 1977), p. 10.
4. Wayne Grudem, *Systematic Theology*, (Leicester, England: Inter-Varsity Press, 1994), p. 558.
5. These would be His incommunicable attributes, such as His omnipresence, omnipotence, and omniscience, for He was completely dependent on the Father and the Holy Spirit.
6. Actually the Synoptic gospels (Matthew, Mark and Luke) speak more of Jesus' compassion than John, but because he was an eyewitness to Jesus' compassion, I felt it was important to include these thoughts on the compassion of Jesus.
7. Charles Spurgeon, "The Great Mystery of Godliness," *Spurgeon's Expository Sermons*, Vol. 3, p. 10.
8. Charles Spurgeon, "The Glory of God in the Face of Jesus Christ," *Twelve Striking Sermons* (London: Marshall, Morgan & Scott, Ltd, 1953), p. 141.
9. Charles Spurgeon, *2200 Quotations from the Writings of Charles Spurgeon*, Tom Carter, comp. (Grand Rapids, MI: Baker Book House, 1988), p. 111.

10. Spurgeon said, "The look which blesses us so as to produce tenderness of heart is a look to Jesus as the pierced One…. It is not looking to Jesus as God only which affects the heart, but looking to this same Lord and God as crucified for us. We see the Lord pierced, and the piercing of our own hearts begins (Charles Spurgeon, "How Hearts Are Softened," *Spurgeon's Expository Encyclopedia,* Vol. 8, p. 377).

Five

The Glory of the Cup

Why Did Jesus Sweat Blood in the Garden?

John's heart trembles even more now as he recalls another expression of God's glory. Only this time, Jesus didn't exude glory from the pores of His skin as He did at His transfiguration; this time He exuded *blood!*

Without a whip, or thorn, or nail to rip through His human flesh, blood pressed out through His skin like oil crushed out of an olive. Emotion surges in the old apostle's heart as he thinks of that night in the Garden of Gethsemane, which means, "garden of crushed olives."

First Issue of the Lamb's Blood

Vividly, he recalls the night he followed the Master out of the city, crossing over the Brook Kidron. Because it was Passover, the waters ran dark red with blood from slain lambs, funneled down from the Temple Mount. Now John knows that Jesus was on His way to become that Passover Lamb, His own blood running like the crimsoned waters of the Kidron.

Presently, they entered Gethsemane. John remembers how the full Passover moon cast silvery glints on the olive leaves. Most of all, he remembers with stabbing pain that Jesus asked him to pray. Jesus cried, *"My soul is overwhelmed with sorrow to the point of death"* (Matthew 26:38), but John fell asleep.

Suddenly, the young disciple awakened, startled by a deep vibration he felt in the ground beneath him. He lifted his head and heard a moaning sound, like an animal howling. No…it was Jesus, praying.

John crawled up closer to the Lord. He blinked and focused his eyes. In the light of the Passover moon, what he saw knocked the wind from his lungs.

Here lay Jesus, the one who contained the glory of Eternity, rolling in the dirt, soaked in His own blood. Clots of blood fell from His body, splotching His robe and pooling on the ground. John's heart twisted, for this was the first issue of the Lamb's blood, offered up as by a high priest in the holy of holies of prayer.

Luke wrote, *"And being in anguish, he prayed more earnestly, and his sweat was like drops of blood falling to the ground"* (22:44). The Greek word for *drops* is *thrombos*, meaning, "large, thick drops of clotted blood."[1]

Jonathan Edwards said Jesus' blood fell to the ground in clots because when it hit the cool night air, it "congealed or stiffened."[2] And though some today try to dismiss this as merely heavy sweat, sweat never congeals to form clots. Only blood thickens when air hits it. This could be nothing else but rich, red human blood, issuing from the veins of the Lamb.

But why? What caused the Savior to sweat great drops of blood? Was it dread of the Roman scourge, embedded with bits of bone and metal, that would rip His human flesh to shreds? Was it fear of thorns gouging His brow or spikes impaling His hands? Did He shrink from the shame and humiliation by His enemies, gawking like hungry hawks at His naked, bleeding body?

Did He quail from the filth of humanity's sin which the Father would dump upon Him? Did the torment of Satan's demons, flinging themselves upon Him, feeding greedily on the sin, make Him cower?

Did He flinch from the sword piercing His side, emptying out every drop of His human blood to the ground? Did the chilling thought of death overwhelm Him? Did the thought of the cold slab of the tomb overpower Him? Many martyrs have courageously hung from crosses or laid their necks on chopping blocks for their faith in God.

Was Jesus more cowardly than these martyrs?

Did He cringe from the grief of losing His Father's presence? To be sure, the abandonment of His Father was horrifying beyond measure. Through all eternity He had dwelt in the *"bosom of the Father"* (John 1:18, KJV) in face-to-face communion as part of the Triune Godhead, but was the thought of this separation what caused blood to rush from His pores and fall in clots to the ground?

I'm asking *you*, why did Jesus' own blood burst out of His pores as He prayed in the garden? Do you know why? What could cause such extreme anguish in the heart of our Lord? The answer is found in His prayer.

Peer again through the olive leaves in the garden and listen.... *"Father,"* He roars, *"if you are willing, take THIS CUP from me"* (Luke 22:42). What then is this cup?

A Revelation of the Cup

These words of Jesus now reel and crash through the recesses of John's brain, as he stands on Patmos gazing up at the Lamb. He sucks in a long, deep breath and holds it. He bites his lip and braces himself, knowing he is about to look into the contents of that cup. He's seen it before, but now the full revelation of it breaks like a summer storm over his tender soul.

He thinks first of what the Old Testament said about this cup. The psalmist warned, *"In the hand of the LORD is a cup full of foaming wine mixed with spices"* (Psalm 75:8). The reason spices were mixed into the brew was to increase its intoxicating effect. This cup in God's hand was *"filled with the wine of MY WRATH"* (Jeremiah 25:15; see Isaiah 51:17). This is ultimately the cup that all who reject Jesus Christ will drink, filled with *"the wine of God's fury,…poured full strength into THE CUP OF HIS WRATH"* (Revelation 14:10).[3]

Jeremiah said that when the nations drink this cup, *"they will stagger and go mad"* (25:16). But John knows that when Jesus drank this cup, He screamed out the cry of madness: *"My God, My God, why have You forsaken Me?"* (Matthew 27:46, NKJ). Theologians today call this the cry of dereliction.[4] Why was such a cry wrenched from the Savior's lips? It was because He had been drinking the CUP OF WRATH![5]

John's shoulders shake. His whole body trembles. Never has this hit him so hard. "Jesus," he cries up to the Lamb, "no wonder the thought of the cup was killing You. You asked me to pray. You said, *"I am almost dying of sorrow"* (Matthew 26:38, AMP). But I couldn't even stay awake! Oh, God, forgive me!"

But, John, there's something far worse than falling asleep before He drank the cup on the cross. In our day, He's already drained the cup, and the Church for whom He drank it still sleeps. We've lost the passion for the cross because we've never really looked into the fiery cup. We don't know what He did for us. Once a year, we talk about nails and whips and blood, but we rarely, if ever, consider the cup.

Have you ever heard a sermon on it?[6] Have you ever read a book about it? Oh, I ask you — why have we so neglected to look into this subject? I believe it is the apex, the crux, the high point of the Bible. It is the climax of His work on the cross. Jonathan Edwards said it was the "principal errand" for which He came to this earth.[7]

A Baptism of Fire

John's heart bursts with grief, but he also feels the heat burning against his face. He knows this is the light for revelation as he dares to look again into the Father's cup.

Suddenly, John sees it. He sees the flames leaping. He sees the bush burning.[8] He sees "fire from heaven" blazing down upon the burnt offering on the altar. He sees the Passover lamb, "roasting" over the flames. He sees the furnace into which Jesus' human body will be cast, which was, said Jonathan Edwards, "vastly more terrible than Nebuchadnezzar's fiery furnace."[9]

There in Gethsemane, said Edwards, "He was brought to the mouth of the furnace that He might look into it, and stand and view its raging flames and see the glowings of its heat, that He might know where he was going and what He was about to suffer."[10]

What was this furnace? It was the eternal wrath of Almighty God, into which the Son would be thrust, while hanging from two strips of wood. This is what Jesus meant when He said, *"I have a baptism to undergo, and how distressed I am until it is completed!"* (Luke 12:50). This was indeed a BAPTISM OF FIRE which He would experience on the cross.

Pain rakes through John's heart as he thinks of the infinite wrath and eternal judgment which filled that cup. Not only this, but God took His eternal wrath, condensed it, and emptied it into His cup. He distilled eternal judgment, the very lake of fire, and poured it into His cup. He placed hell's blazing fury into this cup and asked His Son to drink it.

Jonathan Edwards said that Jesus would endure "the very pains of hell." The contents of this cup were "fully equivalent to the misery of the damned for it was the wrath of the same God."[11] John Stott said, "We may even say that our sins sent Christ to hell," not after the cross but "before His body died."[12]

A.W. Pink said, "Not all the thunderbolts of divine judgment...not all the weeping and gnashing of teeth of the damned in the lake of fire" ever gave such a demonstration "of His infinite hatred of sin as did the wrath of God which flamed against His own Son on the cross."[13]

Now John sees why blood burst out of His skin. It was from a violent inner struggle as He grappled with the horrors of drinking the Father's cup. Edwards said, He was "covered with clotted blood" which "had been forced through His pores through the violence of His agony."[14]

There in the Garden of Gethsemane, the young disciple finally saw the Lord lift His face toward Heaven. With tears pouring from His eyes, love weeping in His heart, and blood squeezing from His pores, Jesus cried: *"Not my will, but yours be done"* (Luke 22:42). Jesus then slumped to the ground, limp and weak, bathed in His own blood. He was exhausted from wrestling in prayer with God, but ready to drink the Father's cup of wrath.

Why Did He Do It?

How could He do it? Why would He surrender to drinking this cup? Do you know why? He wanted to be obedient to His Father, and He knew He must fulfill the eternal Covenant of Redemption; but there was another reason, one so gripping it will melt you in tender devotion.

He could have said "no" and watched the whole human race plummet into hell. But He looked into that furnace of wrath and saw something compelling. It was something beautiful. He would rather go through the flames of hell than let this treasure slip away.

You see, He looked into the furnace of hell and He saw *you*.

He saw you enduring the punishment you deserve for sin. It's not that God is cruel and vindictive, looking for people to punish. But God is holy, and He wants you near Him. Unholiness cannot come into the presence of a holy God. So the Son of God raced down to this earth to throw Himself in front of the Father's eternal wrath. Theologians call this *propitiation,* which means, "a sacrifice to avert wrath."[15]

It's like the story of the mother who awakened one night smelling smoke. She shook her husband and raced upstairs to the baby, but a wall of flames drove her back. Outside, the neighbors and firemen fought the blaze. But the mother kept hearing the cry of her baby from the upstairs window. Her husband held her back, knowing there was nothing they could do.

Finally, she broke from his grip and tore into the house. Covering her face with her hands, she charged up through the wall of flames into her baby's room. Gathering her in her arms, she placed her inside her robe and pressed back through the flames. In a crumpled heap of charred flesh, she fell to the grass outside. And though she was disfigured for life, she had saved her baby.

In a far greater way, that's what Jesus did for *you*. Like the mother who heard the cries of her baby, He heard your cries. He felt your pain and watched you try to numb the ache with sin. Though you didn't know it, He saw you heading toward the flames of an eternal hell.

So He left Heaven and charged through the flames of wrath to rescue you. He took your hell and drank your cup on the cross. He swept you into His arms and brought you through to safety, though He too was disfigured. He still bears scars to show what He did for you.

The Forgotten Story

Do you see how we have neglected the story of the Lamb? Men like Luther, Calvin, Edwards, Spurgeon, Wesley, Pink and others of former generations preached and wrote about this infinite cup of wrath. But this subject, which is the high point of the Bible, the very apex of the cross, has altogether faded from the Church in our generation.

How could this happen? How could we forget what Edwards called "the principal errand" of Jesus' trip to earth? Most of all, how could the Father sacrifice so deeply, only to have us mention the cross once a year at Easter? Even then, we only mention the whip and nails and thorns.

It is my conviction that we have wounded the heart of God by overlooking the depths of His Son's sacrifice. I believe the Father aches to see His Son glorified as the Lamb. Maybe this story will help you feel His heart.

One day a father received the most dreaded phone call a parent could receive. A police officer called to tell him there had been a terrible accident: "I'm sorry, sir, but your son has been killed!"

The father threw on his jacket and rushed to the scene of the accident. But by the time he arrived, his son's body had been removed and most of the wreckage cleared away. All he could see was his son's blood and tissue splattered across the highway.

When he saw the cars driving carelessly over the bloodstains of his son, he jumped from his car and ran to the middle of the road. Tearing off his jacket, he began waving it, flagging cars away. Tearfully, he screamed, *"Don't you know you're traveling over the blood of my son?"*

But that's how God feels when He looks down and sees the way we have trampled the blood of His Son! We have trifled His sacrifice by ignoring the cup His Son drank for us.

Yes, we've whitewashed the truth. Maybe once a year we've sentimentalized over the cross, but we've been oblivious to the magnitude of His suffering. We've turned a deaf ear to His cries. We've slighted the cup of wrath that melted His heart (see Psalm 22:14).

We've tolerated unholiness, not realizing that this drives nails again through His wounds (see Hebrews 6:6, 10:29). We've been preoccupied with material blessings and wondered why a whole generation of young people, because they haven't seen a reason to follow Jesus, slips silently into hell.

Most of all, those of us in ministry have neglected to point to the Lamb. We've failed to preach and teach only *"Jesus Christ and him crucified...with a demonstration of the Spirit's power"* (1 Corinthians 2:2,4). David Wilkerson wrote, "The one thing God will never endure is the casting aside of the preaching of the cross."[16] Spurgeon said, "The minister who has failed to cry, 'Behold the Lamb of God,' may expect at the last to be cut up in pieces and to have his portion with the tormentors."[17]

Where are the Charles Spurgeons of our day who will lift up the Lamb of God? Where are the Jonathan Edwardses who will dig into the depths of theology and unveil the agony of our Lord? Where are the Apostle Pauls who will glory in the cross (see Galatians 6:14)? Where are the broken ones who will bring Him the reward of His suffering?

Every day I walk down to my prayer garden, shaded by a canopy of oak branches, at our camp. I grip the cross in the garden and cry out with all my heart:

O God, raise up a generation whose hearts bleed for the One who bled for them! Though we have neglected Your Lamb, my God, please — for the sake of Your Son — cut to the quick of a whole generation and pierce their hearts with a revelation of the Lamb! Holy Spirit, scar them forever with a revelation of the cup! Then send them out, telling the nations about the One who drank the Father's cup of punishment. Anoint them with the power flowing out from His resurrection so they can bring to the world a revelation of *the Glory of the Lamb!*

Endnotes

1. *Vine's Expository Dictionary of Old and New Testament Words* (Nashville: Thomas Nelson Publishers, 1996), p. 185.
2. Jonathan Edwards, "Christ's Agony," *The Works of Jonathan Edwards,* Vol. 2 (Edinburgh: Banner of Truth Trust, 1995), p. 868.
3. There are several kinds of cups in the Bible, but the cup over which Jesus agonized in the garden was clearly the cup of God's wrath. John Stott wrote: "What is this cup? Is it physical suffering from which He shrinks, the torture of the scourge and the cross, together perhaps with the mental anguish of betrayal, denial and desertion by His friends, and the mockery and abuse of His enemies? Nothing could ever make me believe that the cup Jesus dreaded was any of these things (grievous as they were) or all of them together. His physical and moral courage were indomitable. To me it is ludicrous to suppose that He was now afraid of pain, insult and death." (John R.W. Stott, *The Cross of Christ* [Downers Grove, IL: InterVarsity Press, 1986], p. 74.)

4. John R. W. Stott, *The Cross of Christ*, pp. 78-79.
5. John Stott further describes this cup: "That cup from which He shrank...symbolized neither the physical pain of being flogged and crucified, nor the mental distress of being despised and rejected even by His own people, but rather the spiritual agony of bearing the sins of the world, in other words, of enduring the divine judgment which those sins deserved. That this is the correct understanding is strongly confirmed by Old Testament usage, for in both the wisdom literature and the prophets, the Lord's 'cup' was a regular symbol for wrath." (Stott, *The Cross of Christ*, p. 76)
6. Steve Hill and Leonard Ravenhill are the only preachers I have ever heard talk about the cup in our day.
7. Jonathan Edwards, "Christ's Agony," p. 869.
8. The Father showed Jesus that He would become the burning bush, aflame with God's wrath but not consumed (Exodus 3:2). As Edwards said, "The bush burning with fire, represented the sufferings of Christ in the fire of God's wrath" (Jonathan Edwards, "The History of the Work of Redemption," *The Works of Jonathan Edwards,* Vol. 1 [Edinburgh: Banner of Truth Trust, 1995], p. 546.)
9. Jonathan Edwards, "Christ's Agony," p. 867.
10. Ibid.
11. Ibid., pp. 868, 871.
12. John R. W. Stott, *The Cross of Christ,* p. 79. It is important to know that the hell Jesus endured was all on the cross, not after the cross. One could only believe that He suffered in hell after the cross, if one didn't understand the cup of wrath. Leon Morris would agree, for he defines "hell" as the working out of the wrath of God (Leon Morris, *The Atonement* [Downers Grove, IL: Inter-Varsity Press, 1983], p. 164.) For an excellent work, showing that Christ did not descend into hell for further suffering, see Wayne Grudem, *Systematic Theology* (Leicester, England: InterVarsity Press, 1994), pp. 586-594. Sadly, today, many preachers speak of Jesus going to hell and fighting with the devil, which actually weakens and undermines the message of the cross. Let it be clearly understood that *"having disarmed the powers and authorities, he made a public spectacle of them, triumphing over them by the cross"* (Colossians 2:15).
13. A. W. Pink, *Seven Sayings of Jesus on the Cross* (Grand Rapids, MI: Baker Book House, 1958), p. 72.
14. Jonathan Edwards, "Christ's Agony," p. 869.
15. Wayne Grudem, *Systematic Theology,* p. 580. Leon Morris, *The Atonement* (Downers Grove, IL: InterVarsity Press, 1983), p. 169.

16. David Wilkerson, "They Have Done Away With the Cross!" *Times Square Church Pulpit Series* (New York City, Feb. 23, 1996), p. 2.
17. Charles Spurgeon, "Behold the Lamb of God," *Spurgeon's Expository Encyclopedia,* Vol. 3 (Grand Rapids, MI: Baker Book House, 1977), p. 103.

Six

The Glory of His Love
When the Son Drank His Father's Cup

John's throat feels raw and swollen with emotion from looking so deeply into the cup. Now he hears the four living creatures and the heavenly Sanhedrin singing a new song: *"You are worthy."*

John's heart swells, as he hears them tell why the Lamb is worthy: *"Because you were slain, and with your blood you purchased men for God from every tribe and language and people and nation"* (Revelation 5:9).

No one knows better than John what this means, for he was there. He watched blood stream down Jesus' body. He stood watching Him writhe in agony as He engulfed the Father's cup.

Tears spill from the old apostle's eyes and burn down his cheeks as he thinks of that monumental day — the day God's eternal Lamb drank the Father's cup. No other moment in all human history ever displayed the glory of God's love so magnificently.

Come and See the Lamb

Come now with John to a little hill outside Jerusalem. Stand on the crest of the hill and look up through the eyes of the young disciple. See black clouds billow across the sky, hiding the light of the sun. Watch lightning scorch the darkness, lighting the scene like heavenly floodlights. Feel emotion crackle in the air, charging the atmosphere with sorrow and hatred and love.

Look up now at the face of Jesus. Hear Him wail His last cries. See blood spill from open wounds. But look deeper than the physical pain. This is where we often stop, but let's look higher. Tune your ears above the din of the crowd. Hear beyond the weeping women, scoffing priests, cursing Romans, moaning thieves and groaning earth.

Come now with reverent awe and humble heart to behold the mystery unveiled. Look into the glory of the cup, which is the soul of His suffering.

Draw so near you can almost feel the heat of the burnt offering warming your face. Feel the bush burning against your cheeks until, like Moses, you must slip the shoes from your feet, for you stand on holy ground. Behold now the Lamb as He takes away the sin of the world by drinking His Father's cup.

John closes his eyes. It feels to him as though once again he is there, looking up at Jesus....

Loud cries fill the air. Thunder rumbles in the distance.

John feels the wind flapping his tunic. In his arms he holds Jesus' mother, honored by the Lord to care for her even above her other sons. She trembles against his chest, heaving with grief and unspeakable pain.

John can't take his eyes from the Master. Jesus is a visage of bruised and macerated flesh. Blood and sweat lather His body. Tears and spittle coat His face. His body twists and thrashes under the weight of human sin. Like the brass serpent lifted on a pole (see Numbers 21:9 and John 3:14), He was lifted on the pole of a cross, bearing the poison of sin. God has taken all the sin of the world and crushed it down on Him.

As He writhes under the heavy load, nails tug against His hands. Ropes burn His arms, holding Him to the wood, preventing the nails from ripping through the flesh of His hands. Raw wounds on His back scrape against the rough-hewn wood.

Suddenly, Jesus' body stops writhing. His whole body stiffens. His face pales. His eyebrows lift and His eyes fly open wide.

A look of terror covers His face. His eyes tell the story. They are swollen and red, bulging with tears, filled with untold horror. John has seen that look before in the moonlight of Gethsemane, when Jesus was crying out to His Father about the cup.

As you stand with John now, watch the mouth of the furnace open over the Innocent One. Watch the Passover Lamb roast. See the "fire from Heaven" roar down upon the "burnt offering." See the bush burn with fiery judgment as eternal wrath tumbles down upon the Son. See the lake of fire empty on the Innocent One as hell flames down and wave after wave of punishment crashes against the Lamb.

Understand that this is not simply the wrath of one person's hell. This is the accumulated hell for all humanity. From Adam to the last person conceived on earth, from Adolph Hitler to Saddam Hussein, to you and me, Jesus is taking our punishment for sin.[1]

He is *"stricken by God, smitten by him, and afflicted."* He is *"pierced for our transgressions"* and *"crushed for our iniquities."* Indeed, *"the punishment that brought us peace"* is on Him. *"Oppression and judgment"* are on Him, for *"it was the LORD's will to crush him and cause him to suffer"* (Isaiah 53:4-5, 8,10).

The Father's Pain

John's pulse throbs wildly in his head. His stomach twists and churns. He holds Mary close, hoping to comfort her as the sword pierces into her soul. Grief grinds the young disciple's heart.

He wonders, if his own heart is bursting, how must the heart of the Father feel?

During the Holocaust, a Jewish boy told of having to feed his own father to the flames of a crematorium at Auschwitz, one of Hitler's death camps. How much more it would grieve a father to have to feed his own son to the fire. Yet, what infinite grief it causes the heavenly Father to feed the darling of His heart, His own precious Son, into these horrid flames. Think of it — the Father casts His own beloved Son into the crematorium of Calvary!

God's eternal Son, who communed with Him in face-to-face intimacy through all eternity, is now abandoned by His Father. Father God turns away His face of love and pummels Him with punishment. The pain this brings the Father is fathomless.

Hours pass. Jesus drinks and drinks and drinks.

Finally, He has drained the cup almost down to the last drop. Now something happens that intensifies the grief in the Godhead. Jesus prepares to scream the cry of dereliction into His Father's face. Sorrow fills the Father's heart to infinite proportions.

The Cry of Dereliction

A rush of anguish sweeps over the young disciple. He grips Mary more tightly. Tears blind his eyes. He frees one arm and brushes away the wetness on his cheeks with the back of his hand.

As the ninth hour nears, John sees Jesus push down on the spike in His feet, lifting His chest to take in a lungful of air. His push on the spike opens the wounds in His feet. Blood spurts from beneath the spike, spilling down His feet and toes, dripping down the wood and soaking into the ground.

Jesus turns His gaze upward. John can see the tears quivering in His eyes. The Lord throws back His head. His mouth flies open wide as though He's about to speak. He spoke three times in the first three hours, once to forgive, next to save a dying thief, and third to place His mother into John's care.

In these past three hours, not a word has fallen from His lips. The pain has been too deep for words. The horror of the cup has crushed His breath away. Now, however, He prepares to speak.

John inches a little closer, still holding Mary. For a moment, time stands still. The crowd hushes. Tension charges the atmosphere. Hearts thunder in every breast.

Now, with a deep, guttural, animal-like roar, Jesus shrieks: *"Eli, Eli, lama sabachthani?"* The words are a mixture of Hebrew and Aramaic, John's heart language. He knows they mean, *"My God, My God, why have You forsaken Me?"* (Matthew 27:46, NKJ).

The crowd stands paralyzed. Birds' songs freeze in midair. The wind stops blowing. The sun still hides its face. Dark clouds, heavy with moisture, hang low as though ready to drop a load of tears.

Bolts of shock jolt John's whole body. Jesus' words boom through his fevered brain.

He can hardly believe it. He stood by as the Roman flagellum plowed Jesus' flesh, as thorns were stuck like icepicks into His brow, as spikes were driven through His hands and feet, and as people spat in His face, but *"as a sheep before her shearers is silent, so he did not open his mouth"* (Isaiah 53:7).

Yet now He screams like a wounded animal. He doesn't whimper like a lamb; He roars like a lion. Why?

It's because He's been drinking His Father's cup.[2]

A verse from the Psalms fills John's mind: *"My God, My God, why have You forsaken Me? Why are You so far from helping Me, and from the words of My groaning?"* (Psalm 22:1, NKJ).

Puritan scholar John Flavel said the Hebrew here for *groaning* "comes from a root that signifies, to howl or roar as a lion; and rather signifies the noise made by a wild beast than the voice of a man." "It is as though," said Flavel, "Christ had said, 'O My God, no words can express My anguish: I will not speak but roar, howl out My complaint; pour it out in volleys of groans.'"[3]

The Divine Rupture

All this time Jesus' heart has been swelling and filling with grief. The wrath of God has smashed and beaten against Him, until His heart is ready to burst. Now with the cry of dereliction, wrenched from His lips and shot up in the Father's face, His heart begins to crack.

Jesus' tongue is parched from drinking this fiery cup. Now He hangs His head and groans, *"I thirst"* (John 19:28, KJV). A soldier wets the Lord's lips with posca, a cheap vinegar wine. Then He lifts His voice and shouts triumphantly, *"Tetelestai!"* In the perfect tense, it means, "It is now and will forever remain finished!" (see John 19:30).

With the cup completely consumed, His work on earth is done. The types and prophecies and the Law are fulfilled. Because sin has been fully punished in Him, demons have no more sin on which to feed. Now the Seed of the woman crushes the serpent's head (see Genesis 3:15). It's just as the Bible says, *"And having disarmed the powers and authorities, he made a public spectacle of them, triumphing over them by the cross"* (Colossians 2:15).

Yes, even as the Son completed His work of creation on the sixth day, He finishes His work of redemption with His sixth word. And even as He entered His rest on the seventh day of creation, He is about to enter His rest with His seventh word: *"'Father, into your hands I commit my spirit'"* (Luke 23:46).

And now it happens....

His heart breaks. It ruptures, pouring out blood and water.[4] It is just as the Bible says, *"I am poured out like water....My heart is like wax; it is softened [with anguish] and melted down within me"* (Psalm 22:14, AMP).

Yes, Jesus dies of a broken heart from the agony of drinking His Father's cup.

Do you know what this means? It's not just the severing of a veil in the Temple. It's not just the tearing of a veil in Heaven. It's the ripping of the veil of the Son *Himself.* When the veil of the Temple was torn in two from top to bottom (Matthew 27:51), it was a symbol of the tearing of God the

Son — ripped in two by the hand of God.

John watches in agony as a soldier draws back his spear and plunges it into the side of the Lamb. Mary breaks from John's arms and runs to the stone-cold feet of her Son. John kneels beside her, digging his fingers into the wood of the cross. Then suddenly he feels something warm drop upon his hand.

John looks up to see blood and water, rolling down Jesus' body and splashing on his hand (see John 19:34). He bows his head and closes his eyes, knowing his heart will be forever scarred by a revelation of the Lamb.

Pierced by His Love

Won't you allow Him to scar you too? Won't you lay your heart bare before the Lord and allow the Holy Spirit to plunge in His sword. Ask Him to draw the blade through your soul until you can truly see.

For now you've caught a glimpse of the Lamb. You've seen what drinking your cup did to Jesus. You've heard His horrific cry, and you can never be the same. A veil will be *"stripped off and taken away"* (2 Corinthians 3:16, AMP). Indeed, as Simeon said to Mary, *"A sword will pierce through your own soul also"* (Luke 2:35, AMP), for you will be pierced by the love of the Lamb.

Amy Carmichael was a missionary to India. She had a deep love for Buddhist temple prostitutes, but there was one girl whom she couldn't seem to reach. One day, Amy bared her arm and pulled out a long needle. "I'm going to stab this needle into my arm to show you how much I love you," she told the young woman.

"Oh, no!" objected the girl. "That will hurt you too much!" "Not nearly as much as you are hurting me," she replied. Then she thrust the needle deep into her arm. The girl's heart was pierced to the core when she saw such a demonstration of love. She threw her arms around Amy's neck and sobbed, *"Oh, Amy, I never knew you loved me so much!"*

In a far greater way, that's what Jesus did for you. He was pierced to His heart to show you how much He loves you. The Son came from Glory to take your hell so you could have His Heaven, and it ripped His heart in two.

Think of it — the olive was crushed to pour out the oil of His love. The grape was pressed to spill out His mercy on *you*. The vase was shattered to release the fragrance of His glory on *you*. Like the girl cried to Amy Carmichael, won't you cry to Him: *Oh, Jesus, I never knew You loved me so much!"*

Yes, this is the glory of His love. That's why only at the feet of the Lamb can we really begin to *"grasp how wide and long and high and deep is the love of Christ"* (Ephesians 3:18).

And yet, have you ever questioned His love for you? Have you ever secretly thought, *I know He loves others, but does He really love me?* Oh, please don't wound His love with such a thought. Don't crush His heart again.

Simply lean back now and look up. Say this out loud, "Holy Spirit, how does Jesus feel about me?"

Wait until the answer comes....

I think, if you'll look with the eyes of your spirit, you will see an amazing sight. You'll see Jesus, the Lamb upon the throne, reaching in and pulling back the veil of His flesh.

Look carefully and you'll see it. There it is — a scar chiseled into His heart. This scar speaks volumes. It tells of the glory of His love for *you*. Like the names engraved on the gems in the high priest's breastplate, your name is engraved in the wound of His heart.

Look long and deep at that wound until you finally understand how dear you are to Him. Now open wide and let His love flow in. Let Him take His golden pitcher and pour in the glory of His love. Let Him fill you, wiping away all the wounds etched into your soul.

You see, many wounds scar your heart. The beatings of life have left their marks. Jesus wants to wipe away every scar and leave only one. He wants your heart to be forever scarred by a revelation of *the Glory of the Lamb.*

Endnotes

1. This does not mean, by any means, that all people are saved. The concept of all being saved is a heresy known as universalism. Only those who have knelt at the cross and received Jesus Christ can be saved.

2. About this cup, F.W. Krummacher wrote: "We know what was in the cup. All its contents would have been otherwise measured out to us by divine justice on account of sin. In the cup was the entire curse of the inviolable law, all the horrors of conscious guilt, all the terrors of Satan's fiercest temptations, and all the sufferings which can befall both body and soul. It contained likewise the dreadful ingredients of abandonment by God, infernal agony, and a bloody death, to which the curse was attached — all to be endured while surrounded by the powers of darkness." (F.W. Krummacher, *The Suffering Savior* [Grand Rapids, MI: Kregel Publications, 1947], p. 135.)

3. John Flavel, *The Works of John Flavel*, Vol. 1 (London: Banner of Truth Trust, 1968), p. 41.

4. Physicians today tell us that Jesus may have died of a ruptured heart because John said blood and water issued separately from His side. In heart rupture or failure, the red cells separate from the clear serum, accumulating in the pericardium (the membrane around the heart). Scripturally, we only know for certain that Jesus died when He released His spirit to the Father. This account of the rupture of Jesus' heart is based on medical opinions today and cannot be considered absolute. Leon Morris writes, "William Stroud argued that it means a physically ruptured heart, with the result that the blood 'separates into its constituent parts, so as to present the appearance commonly termed blood and water'" (Leon Morris, *Reflections on the Gospel of John* [Peabody, MA: Hendrickson Publishers, Inc., 2000], pp. 674-675). Dr. Truman Davis states, "There was an escape of watery fluid from the sac surrounding the heart and the blood of the interior of the heart. This is another conclusive postmortem evidence that Jesus died, not the usual crucifixion death by suffocation, but of heart failure due to shock and constriction of the heart by fluid in the pericardium" (C. Truman Davis, "A Physician Looks at the Crucifixion," *Arizona Medicine*, Vol. 22, No. 3, March 1965).

Seven

Resurrection Glory

The Resurrection and Ascension of the Lamb

The old disciple pushes up to his feet and stretches his hands toward Heaven. He joins the worship above, as *"ten thousand times ten thousand and thousands of thousands"* (Revelation 5:11, AMP) of angels sing in adoration to the Lamb of God.

With joy bursting from his heart, John recalls the morning Jesus rose from the dead. From his view of the Lamb in Heaven, he now understands even more about His resurrection. He closes his eyes and dares to imagine what it was like in Joseph's tomb. He can feel warm tears welling in his eyes and pressing against his lids as he pictures the scene.

Glory Floods the Tomb

Here lies the body of Jesus, wrapped in grave clothes. Darkness still shrouds the land as the Morning Star prepares to rise. Now the glory of the Triune Godhead invades the corpse of the Son.[1]

Jesus' heart begins to beat. His eyelids flutter open. And suddenly — power pours out of His pierced-open heart. The whole tomb floods with *the resurrection glory of the Lamb.*

Now the *"Sun of Righteousness"* rises *"with healing in His wings and His beams"* (Malachi 4:2, AMP). Now the *"Dayspring from on high"* (Luke 1:78, NKJ) sheds forth His brilliant rays. Now the *"light of the world"* (John 8:12) fills the tomb with His glory.

John's pulse races and his cheeks warm with the light of the Lamb. He can literally feel resurrection power flooding his own being as he thinks of the risen Lamb.

Yes, because the veil of Jesus' flesh was torn on the cross, now the glory behind the veil is released. Now the rock, struck by God's wrath, pours out a river of resurrection life. Omnipotence pours from these hands once riveted to a cross. Omniscience streams from this "sacred head sore wounded."

And from this heart, once ruptured, pour floods and floods and floods of *resurrection glory.* Like molten lava, bubbling and rising from the heart of the earth, resurrection power erupts from the heart of the Lamb.

The Ascension

Forty days later, Jesus leads them up the Mount of Olives.[2] John's thoughts go there again.…

It's a warm day in late spring. Lilies bloom in the fields. Red and yellow anemones dot the hillside. A light breeze tosses the Master's hair as they climb. Now, even as the glory lifted off the Temple and ascended from the Mount of Olives, He who embodies the glory of God is about to ascend from the Mount of Olives.

From the Bethany side of this mount, Jesus raised Lazarus from the tomb; now He is about to rise up from the tomb of this earth. It is from this mount that Jesus made His triumphal entry into the city; now, from this same mount, He is about to make His triumphal entry into the city of God.

Finally, Jesus stops, turns to face them all, and begins to bless them. John looks up at His hands, as "the hands that bled now bless."[3] Several times before, Jesus had opened His robe and displayed the wounds in His hands and feet and side. "Those wounds," Spurgeon said, "were the memorials of His love to His people."[4]

John's heart warms as he remembers this moment on the hillside. Jesus pushes gently on His feet and begins to rise. Now He who created the laws of nature breaks the law of gravity. As He breezes above the trees, olive leaves shimmer and rustle.

Higher and higher He ascends, shedding blessings from His hands. Like a high priest in the Temple, coming out of the Holy of Holies to bless the people, now God's High Priest Himself blesses His people as He mounts toward the Holy of Holies of Heaven. Finally a cloud covers Him and He vanishes from sight.

The Wounded Son Comes Home

Now as John stands here on Patmos, thinking back to this glorious ascension of the Lord, he wonders what it was like when the King of Glory entered back into Heaven. Meditating on the Scriptures, he closes his eyes and imagines the scene.

Jesus walks up to the ancient gates. Angels stand in awe. "Who is this Holy One, who still bears wounds like a Lamb?" "Why, He's the Son of God!" one gasps. *"Lift up your heads, O you gates; be lifted up, you ancient doors, that the King of glory may come in"* (Psalm 24:7).

Now John pictures Jesus, the wounded Son, striding through the gates and into the open court. Angels stand aghast, awed that One so holy could still bear wounds, like medals of honor pinned upon His flesh. Spurgeon said, "Christ wears these scars in His body in heaven as his ornaments. The wounds of Christ are His glories...they are His jewels and His precious things."[5]

Jesus is unaware of the stares of heavenly beings, for His eyes are fixed on a goal. He sees the One for whom He's been longing. There He is — His Father — waiting with outstretched arms. The look of love on God's face is indescribable.

With purpose and passion, the Son heads straight for His Father's arms. Excitement so fills His heart that He almost stumbles. Seraphim stand aside as He reaches the throne and falls into His Father's arms. At last the wounded Son is home.

And now the wave bursts over the shores of their hearts. It's as though the loneliness of separation, the agony of suffering, the horror of drinking the cup, the relief of completing the work, the joy of releasing the resurrection power, and the love of reunion have all rolled together in one swelling wave of emotion. They weep and weep in each other's arms.

All Heaven stands in hushed silence — not a sound, not a breath, only the muffled sobs of Father and Son.

Timeless moments pass. Then finally the Father opens His arms and stands up straight. He steps to the side and points toward His Son. With triumphant love bursting in His heart, He thunders through Infinitude: *"Behold the Lamb, slain before the creation of the world!"* (see 1 Peter 1:20-21; Revelation 13:8).

As He speaks, resurrection glory pours from the heart of the Lamb.

Excavating the Gospel

Now the Father looks down on planet earth today. He sees the veil that covers the eyes of many Christians, blinding us from seeing His Son as the Lamb. He sees how the cross of His Son has been relegated to a cob-webbed corner in the basement of many churches, only brought out once a year. He sees how other churches neglect *"the power outflowing from His resurrection"* (Philippians 3:10, AMP). I believe His heart aches to see His Beloved One honored as the Lamb.

It's somewhat like the story of the Armenian father whose

son's school was flattened in a magnitude 8.2 earthquake which struck Armenia in 1989, killing 30,000 people. The father rushed to the school, where he found parents screaming over their children who had been crushed to death beneath the rubble. He stood in shock until he remembered his promise to his son: "Armand, no matter what, I'll always be there for you!"

Racing around to the part of the school where his son's classroom once stood, he began digging. For eight hours he dug with his bare hands, stone by stone, handful by handful. People came and said it was hopeless. The fire chief told him to stop, for fires were breaking out everywhere. But he refused to quit. He kept gouging and scooping until his hands were torn and his fingers bleeding.

On through the night he dug, twelve hours, twenty-four hours, thirty-six. His hands ached, but he wouldn't give up. Finally, in the thirty-eighth hour, he lifted a heavy boulder and thought he heard his son's voice. "Armand?" he screamed. "Dad…? Dad, I knew you'd come! You promised you'd always be there for me!"[6]

Yes, a boy was excavated by a father determined to keep his word to his son. How much more will God the Father keep His word to His beloved Son.

He will indeed excavate Him from the rubble in the Church. He will dig out the debris of greed, the stones of materialism, the mudslides of religion, and the boulders of pride and legalism that have blocked our vision of the Lamb.

He won't give up until His Son receives the glory He deserves for giving His life as the Lamb.

Revealing God's Son as the Lamb

I think I know a little of how the Father feels, for I have held this yearning in my heart for two decades. In the mid 1980s, I visited a Methodist Sunday school class, where a man said, "So what's the big deal about Jesus dying on a cross? Lots of people have died on crosses and we don't worship them!" Members of the class came to Jesus' defense, describing the pain of whip and nails and the grief of separation from His Father.

My heart was bursting. I had been teaching a "Life of Christ" course in a Bible college and I had been ravished by reading Jonathan Edwards and other scholars on the Father's cup of wrath. I couldn't contain myself, so finally I poured out my heart.

I said, "It wasn't just the pain of nails and whip or the suffering of physical pain. It wasn't only the grief of separation from the Father, as terrible as this was. We've all had times when God's presence lifted, but it didn't cause us to sweat blood." I explained, "No, that which caused Him to squeeze out blood from His pores in the garden and wrenched from His lips on the cross, *My God, why have You forsaken Me?* was the Father's cup of wrath. This is what sets His cross above all others." Then with deep emotion, I cried, "No man has ever suffered the pangs of eternal wrath and hell, all condensed into this cup! He took your hell so you could have His Heaven!"

They invited me to come back and teach the class, but it's what happened to me in church that transformed me forever. I sat in the pew, weeping and shaking under the power of God. I felt His Spirit flaming down upon me. I had been a Pentecostal Christian for decades, but never had I experienced the pure blazing power of the Holy Ghost like I did that day. As I sat in church, I made a commitment to God. I promised Him that for the rest of my life, I would study and write and teach and preach the cross of Jesus Christ.

For years I taught and wrote books and preached on the cross, the cup and the Lamb. My heart ached with an indescribable longing to see the Son glorified as the Lamb. Once a publisher sneered, "You make me sick! You made me look at the blood and gore of the cross, and I'm repulsed!" I was crushed but not daunted. Like the father at the earthquake rubble, I just kept digging. I couldn't imagine how the Father could allow His Son's sacrifice, which is so honored in Heaven, to be so neglected here on earth.

I went on to study in seminary, and once I heard a professor say, "It wouldn't have mattered if Jesus had died of a heart attack!" I shot out of my seat in front of hundreds of younger students, and cried, "Oh, no, sir! That's not right!" I started telling him about the Father's cup, which the professor casually dismissed.

Once again I was crushed, not for my feelings, but for

God's. I couldn't understand how God could sacrifice so much and people could remain so blind. I was desperately hungry to see the Son glorified as the Lamb.

In 1995, while still in seminary, I stepped into the river of revival at Ché Ahn's Harvest Rock Church in Pasadena, California. After the power of God knocked me to the floor, I sat up and had a brief glimpse of Jesus. I saw Him standing in Heaven like a Lamb, with floods and floods and floods of revival pouring out from Him. This scripture came to me: *"He will come like a pent-up flood that the breath of the Lord drives along"* (Isaiah 59:19). This only deepened my yearning to see the Son of God glorified as the Lamb.

Even after founding a revival camp near Pensacola and teaching courses at the revival school, the ache in my heart continued. Often I would walk through my prayer garden at the camp, crying out to God, "When will You unveil to Your people the magnitude of Your Son's sacrifice? When will You show them the cup? I feel it so deeply, but I know Your heart must ache so much more. Oh, when will You reveal Your Son as the Lamb?"

What I didn't know was that Mel Gibson was already planning to bring forth his movie, "The Passion of the Christ," which the Lord would use to rip veils away from the eyes of the Church and to strike the hearts of millions. I also didn't realize that the Holy Spirit had begun, quietly and imperceptibly, to unveil a revelation of God's Son as the Lamb to so many of my students. Stories started pouring in which showed the fruit.

Stories of Fruit

After Christmas break, Ronald ran up to me with a huge grin on his face. "Dr. Sandy," he cried, "my atheistic aunt was dying, and no one could ever get through to her with the plan of salvation." With overflowing joy, he said, "I prayed with her on her deathbed, describing Jesus as the Lamb with blood streaming from His wounds, and she saw it! That was the moment of breakthrough, and shortly after she got saved!"

During the summer, Katie called me, bursting with excitement. She told me about her mother, who had criticized her for witnessing. One day her mom said, "How dare you impose your beliefs on others!" Katie explained how difficult it is to witness, knowing her reputation would probably be stripped. Then she tearfully described Jesus' sacrifice, concluding, "If my sin cost Him His life, then at least let my life cost me my reputation!" Her mother was so stunned that she began to embrace her daughter's message herself.

I received a letter from Jamie and Yolanda, a young couple from England who had visited here, drinking deeply from the revival and the revelation of the Lamb. One day the spirit of revelation came on Jamie, showing him Isaac's question to his father, as he was about to be sacrificed on the mount. Isaac cried, *"Father,… where is the lamb?"* (Genesis 22:7). Suddenly, Jamie saw his own young generation as an Isaac generation, starving for a deeper revelation of Jesus, crying out, "Father, where's the Lamb?"

Back in England, he shared this revelation with his pastor, and suddenly the Holy Spirit came upon the pastor, healing his back which had been seriously hurt that morning. Yolanda wrote me and said, "We were so excited that God just moved as we glorified His Lamb!"

Pastor Clay, whose daughter, Mary, had been saved when she came here for a "holiday," called to tell me what happened the night she had first received a revelation of the Lamb (story in chapter two). That same night she e-mailed her father:

> Dad, we need to see the blood of the Lamb.... He thought of you when His face was beaten until it was disfigured. He thought of you when His beard was torn and ripped out of His face, when His back was torn apart and His flesh was gouged.... If we could only comprehend God's wrath, which Jesus drank for us. He came down from Heaven, stepped out from eternity, so He could drink our punishment. Eternal, never-ending punishment for our sins.... Dad, I can't find words to explain it....

Shortly afterward, this pastor, while ministering in the Ukraine, read his daughter's letter at the end of his message. When they heard these simple words, describing the

Lamb, they began to weep and run to the altar. A fresh wind of holiness blew out over them all as they gave themselves to the bleeding Lamb of God.

One year after her conversion, Mary, this same nineteen-year-old from England, stood before one thousand people in a Bulgarian church, preaching about the Lamb. She told how Jesus carried all of her sin and then the Father poured down on Him the hell which she deserved. As she spoke, her heart trembled with passion for the Lamb. The passion flowing from her caused other hearts to tremble. The pastor was so broken by her words that he rushed up and gave a tearful altar call. People flooded the altar, hungry to know the Lamb of God and to receive a touch of His resurrection power.

These are only a few of the stories students tell, and I cannot express to you the joy this gives me as Jesus receives the reward of His suffering. For it's not about building big ministries; it's not about having great fame; it's not about accumulating vast fortunes. It's about pouring into the next generation until Jesus receives the glory He deserves for giving Himself as the Lamb.

A Revelation to Your Generation

So where are those who will shoulder the shovel and dig out the rubble that covers God's Son as the Lamb?

Would you be that man or woman? Will you bring a revelation of the Lamb to your generation? Will you reach up to soothe the heart of God?

If so, then fall to your knees and cry out:

O God, I will let Your cup of punishment burn deep in my heart until I am broken by Jesus' brokenness! Then with all my heart I will honor the blood of Your Son! I will reverence His sacrifice! I will tell of Your blazing cup! I will display Your power! With every breath that I take I will live to bring a revelation of Your Son as the Lamb to my generation!

Now look up and behold the pierced Son of God. Gaze upon Jesus until He floods the tomb of your soul with the *resurrection Glory of the Lamb.*

Endnotes

1. Father, Son and Holy Spirit in resurrection: Paul described the Holy Spirit as *"the Spirit of him who raised Jesus from the dead"* (Romans 8:11). Other texts tell us that the Father raised Jesus from the dead (see Acts 2:24; Romans 6:4; 1 Corinthians 6:14; Galatians 1:1; Ephesians 1:20). Yet Jesus described Himself as participating in His resurrection (see John 10:17-18), for He is *"the resurrection and the life"* (John 11:25). Therefore, it is best to conclude that all three persons of the Trinity were involved in the resurrection.

2. Luke wrote, in Luke 24:50 *"When he had led them out to the vicinity of Bethany, he lifted up his hands and blessed them."* But in Acts 1:12, he wrote, *"Then they returned to Jerusalem from the hill called the Mount of Olives."* This is not a discrepancy. Actually, Jesus led them up the Mount of Olives and over to the Bethany side of the mount. Here from Bethany Jesus had raised Lazarus from the tomb; now here from the Bethany side of the hill,

Jesus was getting ready to raise Himself from the tomb of this earth.

3. Charles Spurgeon, "Our Lord's Attitude in Ascension," *Spurgeon's Expository Encyclopedia,* Vol. 4 (Grand Rapids, MI: Baker Book House, 1977), p. 419.
4. Charles Spurgeon, "Evidence of Our Lord's Wounds," (Internet: www.Spurgeon.org).
5. Charles Spurgeon, "The Wounds of Jesus," (Internet: www.Spurgeon.org).
6. Jack Canfield and Mark Victor Hansen, *Chicken Soup for the Soul* (Deerfield Beach, FL: Health Communications, Inc., 1993), pp. 273-274.

Eight

Exaltation Glory
Unveiling the Eternal Glory of the Lamb

A flood of warm tears fills John's eyes as he sees the Lamb receiving the worship He deserves in Heaven. Multitudes of angels say in a loud voice, *"Deserving is the Lamb, Who was sacrificed, to receive all the power and riches and wisdom and might and honor and majesty (glory, splendor) and blessing!"* (Revelation 5:12, AMP).

"Oh, Jesus, now at last You are receiving the glory You deserve for giving Your life as the Lamb!" John cries.

He looks back up to Jesus, standing like a shining orb, lighting all of Heaven with His glory. With worship mounting in his heart, John thinks what it must have been like in Heaven when Jesus sat down on the throne of God at the Father's right hand. His thoughts turn now to that glorious moment in Eternity.

The Victorious Lamb

Jesus has just come from a cross of agony to a throne of glory. Now He takes His place again upon the throne. But this time, something is different: He now inhabits glorified flesh. He is the God-Man on the throne.

Profound thoughts sparkle through John's mind. To think — Jesus went from wearing a cruel crown of thorns to wearing a golden crown of glory! From robes dipped in blood to a kingly robe of splendor! From a mock scepter in His hand to a scepter of authority! From the insults of men to the worship of angels! From the filth of sin to the beauty of holiness! From abandonment by the Father to face-to-face fellowship with the Father! From drinking the Father's cup of wrath to drinking in the fullness of His presence!

No wonder every created being in Heaven and on earth cries out *"To Him Who is seated on the throne and to the Lamb be ascribed the blessing and the honor and the majesty (glory, splendor) and the power (might and dominion) forever and ever (through the eternities of the eternities)!"* (Revelation 5:13, AMP).

John looks up at Him now. Amazement fills his mind. From the victim to the victor! From a worm to a warrior! From humiliation to glorification! From tortured to triumphant! From degradation to exaltation! From a lowly bleeding Lamb to a glorified Lion-Lamb!

This is Heaven's highest glory: that He who sits on High would stoop so low! That He who was *"in very nature God…humbled himself and became obedient to death—even death on a cross!"* (Philippians 2:6,8).

Therefore God exalted him to the highest place and gave

him the name that is above every name, that at the name
of Jesus every knee should bow, in heaven and on earth
and under the earth, and every tongue confess that Jesus
Christ is Lord, to the glory of God the Father.

Philippians 2:9-11

The Glorified Lamb

Now, as He takes His place at the right hand of the Father, the exalted Son slowly lifts His arms. Suddenly, streams of splendor shine out from the Lamb. Every wound bleeds glory. For He is indeed *"the sole expression of the glory of God [the Light-being, the out-raying or radiance of the divine]"* (Hebrews 1:3, AMP).

John falls backward to the rocks, overcome by such revelation of divine glory.

Now the prayer of Jesus is answered, *"Father, glorify me in your presence with the glory I had with you before the world began"* (John 17:5). And now all Heaven explodes with worship, and the four living creatures cry, *"Amen!"* The elders of the heavenly Sanhedrin fall prostrate before the Lamb, worshiping *"Him who lives forever and ever"* (Revelation 5:14, AMP).

Yes, even as *the Glory of the Lamb* flooded on and on through Infinitude before the world's creation, now the sweet light of the Lamb fills Eternity once again. From everlasting to everlasting, His glory shines out. From alpha to omega, from beginning to end, from Eternity to Eternity, He was and is and is to be God's exalted *Lamb of Glory.*

This glory has always flooded beyond the realms of the created world, but for a brief moment, God stepped down from Eternity into time and space. He came to this planet and walked on the ground of the earth. Then He spilled out blood onto the ground.

Think of it — the immortal, invisible, only wise God spilled out blood upon this earth! He who dwells in unapproachable light clothed Himself in the rags of human flesh and allowed that flesh to be torn to shreds. He who is *"the sole expression of the glory of God"* allowed Himself to be impaled on a cross where He drank down every drop of the Father's cup of wrath.

Now do you see? This is why He is *"the Light-being, the out-raying or radiance of the divine."* This is why Habakkuk wrote, *"His brightness was like the sunlight: rays streamed from His hand, and there [in the sunlike splendor] was the hiding place of His power"* (Habbakkuk 3:4, AMP).

This is why Malachi said that *"the Sun of Righteousness"* shall *"arise with healing in His wings and His beams"* (Malachi 4:2, AMP). And this is why *"by his wounds we are healed"* (Isaiah 53:5), for our wounds are healed in His.

The Fountain

Breathless and amazed, John leans back on the rocks, overwhelmed by *the Glory of the Lamb*. He recalls again the glory He saw spilling out of the flesh of Jesus on the Mount of

Transfiguration. Now this innate glory of the Lord has been released from the container of His incarnate flesh.

He remembers the veil in the Tabernacle, through which the glory had filtered and soaked into the Presence bread on the table in the Holy Place (see Numbers 4:7).[1] Now that veil has been ripped apart in the tearing of Jesus' flesh, and His glory shines out through all Eternity.

Clearly, John understands: *"What once had splendor [the glory of the Law in the face of Moses] has come to have no splendor at all, because of the overwhelming glory that exceeds and excels it [the glory of the Gospel in the face of Jesus Christ]."* For if the Law came with glory that faded, *"how much more must that which remains and is permanent abide in glory and splendor!"* (2 Corinthians 3:10-11, AMP).

This is why Paul wrote, *"For God Who said, Let light shine out of darkness, has shone in our hearts so as [to beam forth] the Light for the illumination of the knowledge of the majesty and glory of God [as it is manifest in the Person and is revealed] in the face of Jesus Christ (the Messiah)"* (2 Corinthians 4:6, AMP).

John recalls the words of Jesus, which he didn't understand at the time: *"Do you bring in a lamp to put it under a bowl or a bed? Instead, don't you put it on its stand? For whatever is hidden is meant to be disclosed, and whatever is concealed is meant to be brought out into the open"* (Mark 4:21-22). Now John realizes that because Jesus has been crucified, resurrected and glorified, the light in the lamp shines out. That's why it is said: *"The city does not need the sun or the moon to shine on it, for the glory of God gives it light, and the LAMB IS ITS LAMP"* (Revelation 21:23).

John sees these radiant streams rushing out from the Lamb, causing Him to look like a fountain of light and life. Again, it's just as David said, *"You cause them to drink of the stream of Your pleasures. For with You is the fountain of life; in Your light do we see light"* (Psalm 36:8-9, AMP).

The old apostle knows with all his heart that the reason these rivers of light pour from the Lamb of God, is because the Fountain was opened up at Calvary. These words from an old Welsh hymn help to describe it:

> On the Mount of Crucifixion
> Fountains opened deep and wide;
> Through the floodgates of God's mercy,
> Flowed a vast and gracious tide:
>
> Grace and love, like mighty rivers,
> Poured incessant from above,
> And Heaven's peace and perfect justice
> Kissed a guilty world in love.

Now in Heaven the glorified Lamb is the central focus of every eye. He's the One who lifts His arms and glory explodes from His glorified human flesh. He's the centerpiece of all Heaven. John knows that the very air in Heaven floods with glory. Seraphim drink it in, and all they can do is cry, *"Holy,*

holy, holy" (see Isaiah 6:3; Revelation 4:8).

Worshipers bask in it, but there is only one thing that makes Heaven Heaven. It's the One from whom the glory flows. He's the central Sun of the universe. He's the Chandelier of Heaven, the Daystar of Eternity, God's exalted *Lamb of Glory.*

"*Worthy Is the Lamb!*"

Sometimes, in the midst of worship at Brownsville, I feel almost like John must have felt. The presence of the Lord rolls in and I sense Him pouring over my heart. But it's when we sing about the Lamb and His blood that I enter beyond the veil. As our beloved former pastor, John Kilpatrick, used to say, "The Lord always kisses songs about the blood with a special measure of His presence."

These are the times when my face burns with the light from His face. I can hear the Holy Spirit so clearly when I'm standing in His presence. His presence permeates every portion of my being. I can almost reach up and touch the marks in His flesh.

On a warm Sunday morning in early February 2003, Lindell Cooley was leading the church in the Lord's Supper. He said, "You may have noticed that we're speaking a whole lot more about the blood and the cross at Brownsville."

My heart leapt as he said, "I know I used to sing songs about how much I need the Lord. But there's only one thing

I know that is eternal. It's the cross and the blood of Jesus!" Then he said with passion, "God forgive us if we're more excited about what we want the Lord to do for us, when He's already died for us! If you're not excited about the cross, you need a fresh baptism of Jesus! You need to get saved!"

He smiled his big, boyish grin, and said, "You may be all dressed up this morning and looking nice. But our Father sent a Son from Paradise — from a land of perfection — to a filthy stable."

"Oh, Lord," he cried, looking up to God, "may my eyes never be dry from looking at the cross! May my heart never be cold about what You did for me! I was a child of hell! I belonged in hell! But the merciful, nail-scarred hand of Jesus reached across the abyss and saved me!"

Lindell has moved into his own ministry now, but the presence of God flows on at Brownsville. To me, it's like the worship blows the roof off the sanctuary, as Tony Hooper and the band and choir lead us in glorious worship of the Lamb.

And isn't that just like the Lord? Like David, using the Levites to bring back the ark (see 1 Chronicles 15), He's using the Levites — worshipers — to help carry the ark back to the center of the Church. Like Jehoshaphat, who sent the praisers out front (see 2 Chronicles 20), He's using the praisers to help lead the way into His presence. Like the worshipers in Solomon's Temple (see 1 Kings 8), He's using the worship leaders to help bring in the glory. They are bringing us into the Holy of Holies where we will behold the Lamb.

As we behold the Lamb, His glory will flood down upon us like the light streaming down from the sun. And as His glory pours down, we will behold the Lamb more clearly. At long last, God's Son will receive the glory He deserves for giving His life as the Lamb. Perhaps this story will help explain what I'm trying to say.

The Great Musician

One day a young musician entered a cathedral in Europe. Respectfully he listened as an old organist played on a valuable organ. Then the young musician asked if he might play. The old man was reluctant, not knowing this stranger. Finally, the young man persuaded him and he sat down to play.

Suddenly, the cathedral swelled with the most exquisite music ever played within its walls. With tears in his eyes, the old organist laid his hand on the young man's shoulder and asked, "Who are you?"

"Mendelssohn," came the reply. The old man gasped, for he realized that the greatest musician in the world had just played on his organ and he had almost missed it.

But there is another great Musician waiting in the wings of Heaven. He's the Maestro of Eternity. He played His magnum opus on a little hill outside Jerusalem. The instruments were made of thorns and whip and nails. The symphony came from His heart.

The Father was the Composer, the Holy Spirit was the Conductor, the angels were the silent choir, but the Son was the lone Musician. His cries were the song, His flesh the tablet on which the music was scored.

Now He wants to fill His Church with the music of His glory, but it won't happen until He is allowed to take His rightful place in the Church. When at last we begin to worship the Lamb of God, to preach the Lamb of God, to teach the work of the Lamb of God — then His resurrection glory will fill the sanctuary with the most exquisite strains of music ever heard on earth.

Yes, when at last the Church truly honors the Lamb, then the very worship of Heaven will come down. Then the very prayer of Jesus will be answered: *"Your kingdom come,... on earth as it is in heaven"* (Matthew 6:10). Throne room scenes will be seen on earth, and at the center of it all will be a humble, wounded Lamb, the God-Man who looks like a Lamb.

Indeed, the Church will shine with the glory of God. Just as Jesus prayed, His glory will make us one so that the people of the world will know who He is (see John 17:20-24). Then at last, they will understand the fullness of what God did for them.

At last they will know — He didn't just "die on a cross," like so many thousands of martyrs. His crucifixion was different from the death of any person who ever lived or died, for God's only Son drank down every gruesome drop of His Father's judgment. And because He engulfed eternal hell, now they can be engulfed in the eternal bliss of Heaven. Because He took their punishment, now they can have His peace (see Isaiah 53:5). Because He drank the Father's cup of wrath, now they can drink from His fountain of glory. Because His heart burst open with sorrow, now their lives can overflow with the resurrection power of the Lamb.

This is the message that will bring in the greatest harvest of souls the world has ever known. It's the simple, heart-wrenching, life-changing truth of the Lamb, God's *exalted Lamb of Glory.*

Beholding Him

Of course, we won't fully see the Lamb until we stand in our new bodies in Heaven. But we can dare to look through the windows of the Scriptures and picture that glorious scene.

So before you read the final chapter, let's come one more time and behold the *Lamb of Glory*.

Come beyond the Outer Court, filled with tens of thousands of worshiping angels. Come into the Holy Place with the worshiping elders. Come further now, into the very Holy of Holies through the blood of the Lamb (see Hebrews 10:19).

See multicolored radiance filling the room. See a kaleidoscope of colors encircling the throne. Hear rumbles of thunder. Watch flashes of lightning bolting through the heavenly realms (see Revelation 4:3, 5).

See burning seraphim surrounding the Lord. These are the flaming ones, those closest to the throne. They cover their faces with their wings, for they cannot even bear to look upon the blazing glory and holiness of the Lamb (see Isaiah 6:2; Revelation 4:8).

Now let the glory of God draw your gaze to this One from whom the glory flows. He is the generating force, the source of the glory of God. He is the Headwaters, the Wellspring, the Fountainhead of Glory.

With the eyes of your spirit, look.... Can you see Him there? He looks like *"a Lamb standing, as though it had been slain"* (Revelation 5:6, AMP). He's the Darling of Heaven crucified, the resurrected God-Man, the Omnipotent One who offered Himself as a Lamb.

See His head and His hair, once soaked in blood, now dazzling white as snow. See the One whose eyes once spilled teardrops of sorrow, now blazing like fire. See the face, once swollen and raw from patches of His beard torn out, now radiating brighter than the light of the sun. See His body, once stripped naked and bathed in blood, now bathed in eternal majesty (see Revelation 1:14).

Focus more intently and look at His hands and feet. See the hands that bled from nail holes, now bleeding with infinite splendor (see Habakkuk 3:4). See the feet once spiked to a stake of timber, now gleaming like polished brass (see

Revelation 1:15). See His side, once stabbed with the blade of a spear, now releasing rivers of revival to this earth (see Revelation 22:1-2). Most of all, look at His heart, from which His resurrection glory flows. See the Headwaters of Glory, and hear Him say, "This wound in My heart is for *you.*"

Now come to the waters and drink, for you have allowed Him to pierce the veils on your soul by a long, steady gaze at the Lamb. Because of this, your heart is wide open to receive from the fullness of God.

So drink your fill of this river of glory; then pour it back on Him. For even as a river always seeks to flow back to its source in the ocean, the glory flows from Him and through Him and back to Him.

It is just as the Bible says: *"From him and through him and to him are all things"* (Romans 11:36). That's why this river ultimately flows backwards, leading you back to the heart of Jesus, the source of *the Glory of the Lamb.*[2]

Endnotes

1. After seven days, the priests were supposed to eat this show-bread, or Presence bread. One would think that this bread would be stale after sitting in the open air for a week, but Hebrew tradition holds that the bread was even fresher than the day it was baked. This is because the bread had been soaking up the rays of shekinah light which filtered through the veil into the Holy Place.

2. One morning Pastor John Kilpatrick, who has now stepped into his apostolic calling, shared a dream with the congregation. He said that in the dream he saw a river flowing backwards. My personal interpretation of this dream was that, just as rivers seek to flow back to their source in the ocean, the river of God's glory, which He is soon to pour out, will flow out from Him, but it will also flow backwards — back to the Lamb, for He is the Source of the glory.

Nine

The Glory He Deserves

Glorifying the Son for Becoming the Lamb

With trembling hands and blazing heart, tears swimming in his eyes, the old apostle reaches up and cries, "Why me, Lord? Why not Peter or Paul or James? Why have You let me live to see this vision of the Lamb?"[1]

Suddenly, John looks at the Lamb and knows. It's not because he was the youngest disciple; nor is it because he laid his head on the Master's breast. The reason John is given this revelation of the Lamb is because he was the only one of the Twelve to stand at the foot of the cross.

Of all the disciples, only John risked his life to follow Jesus to that blood-stained hill outside Jerusalem. He saw the Son writhing under the filth of human sin. He watched Him swallow down every scorching drop of the Father's cup. He felt his own heart rip open as he heard Jesus scream, *"My God, My God, why have You forsaken Me?"*

He saw the cold metal of the soldier's spear drive into His side. He watched the blood and water pouring from the gash. He experienced His resurrection glory and looked into

His wounds in the Upper Room. He later watched Him ascend into Heaven, still shedding blessings from His scarred hands.

Yes, the reason John was allowed to see this grand revelation of the Lamb in Heaven is because He was the disciple who had a revelation of the Lamb on earth.

Why Didn't Anyone Tell Me?

One night I read this book to another group of young men and women. After we finished the chapters on the cup, most of them were on the floor weeping. Later they expressed this frustration, saying, "Why didn't anyone ever tell us about this?"

It's somewhat like the story of the young man, blind his whole life, who had an operation and was suddenly able to see. Now that he could appreciate beauty, his mother took him to the shores of the ocean, where he looked out across the vast expanse of the waters and watched the whitecaps foam over the sand. She took him to the mountains, where he saw snowcapped peaks and watched an eagle catch the wind with his wings to rise and circle majestically through the sky. She took him to the forest, where he watched streams cut through the woods and gazed upon towering redwoods.

All this time, the boy's eyes were wide with wonder, but he said very little. Finally, in tears of anger, he burst out, "Why didn't anyone tell me how beautiful it all is?"

Is that how you feel? Does frustration rise within you

when you realize there was so much about the cross you never saw — so much you've never been told about the core of the Christian faith?

If this is how you feel, then I charge you, in the name of Jesus Christ—*you tell them!* You write the books; you paint the pictures; you compose the songs; you develop the videos and movies; you create dramas; you teach the classes; you preach the sermons.

But when you do, tell them what Jesus did as the Lamb. Turn people's ears into eyes. Paul wrote: *"Before your very eyes Jesus Christ was clearly portrayed as crucified"* (Galatians 3:1). The Greek for *portrayed* is *prographō*, which means, "to paint a picture and lift it up on a public placard *'before your very eyes.'"* Said John Stott, "One of the greatest arts or gifts in preaching is to turn people's ears into eyes, and to make them *see* what we are talking about."[2]

Whether by preaching or painting or singing, let people see His blood trickling down His face. Let them feel the whip and thorns, the spikes and spear mutilating His flesh. Let them hear His cries rend the skies. Let them sense the pain tearing open His heart. Let them feel the emotion, the passion, the glory.

Most of all, show them the cup of wrath and hell which He so painfully devoured. Let them see Him groveling in the dirt of Gethsemane, grappling with the horror of drinking His Father's cup until clots of blood covered His body.

Show them the contents of this cup. Let them see the flames of hell which He consumed.

Cause them to feel the Father's heart of anguish as He punished His Beloved One. Let them feel the agony of separation between Father and Son. Let them see the cup of wrath which Jesus transformed into a cup of blessing. Let them see and experience the resurrection power flooding from His heart.

This is what the world waits to see. They need to see a real Jesus, One who drips tears, spills blood, feels pain, exudes mercy, gives hope, saves their souls, and pours out His power upon them. So show them an authentic God who became a Lamb.

If it grieves you that you didn't know until now, then I charge you: don't let another century pass. Don't let another generation fade off the scene without unveiling *the Glory of the Lamb.*

Students Tell the Story

I can hardly contain the joy I've felt watching students express this story of the Lamb in many creative ways.

Four of my students spent at least thirty hours each, piecing together clips from various Jesus movies. They showed whips tearing, nails gouging, blood dripping, people screaming, and Jesus weeping. Following these scenes of the crucifixion flashed pictures of children suffering, people dying, false religions deceiving, and war exploding. Then came the silent question: *"Will you preach Jesus Christ and Him cruci-fied to a lost and dying world?"* We were all gripped by this stunning question.[3]

Another student, Joseph, made a video showing Jesus as the Lamb, bleeding on the cross. He superimposed an im-age of Him over the Wailing Wall in Israel. It was a power-ful demonstration of Jesus' love for Israel as He dripped tears over His Jewish people.

In one of my classes, Patti wrote a song about the heart of Jesus breaking open on the cross. She sang it with her gui-tar and our own hearts melted. Cathy wrote a powerful song about the Father's cup. I heard her sing it in a church in England, and the presence of God flooded the whole sanc-tuary as she sang about the Lamb. Pearlcya painted a pic-ture of a literal lamb on the altar, blood flowing down from its wounds. In the background was a father, pouring wrath down upon the lamb as smoke ascended heavenward.

A middle-aged student, Ron, came out to our camp and built a prayer garden with a massive cross, torches and a waterfall flowing down from the cross. I've stood back and watched our revival students present dozens of dramas, dis-playing a revelation of the Lamb to hundreds of young people, in this beautiful prayer garden. I've seen teenagers' eyes widen as they watched Ryan or Victor, playing the part of Jesus, being beaten, kicked and crucified. Then "Jesus" would climb off the cross and preach his heart out to the young people, "blood" spilling down his body and dripping from his hands.

One night, Ryan stepped down from the cross, showing a group of teenagers his hand filled with "blood." *"Your blood is on my hands!"* he cried. I watched a seventeen-year-old boy, who'd taken drugs on the bus as he rode with his youth group to our camp, look at Ryan's hand. Suddenly he burst into racking sobs. He saw the blood of Jesus, and it pierced his heart. He repented deeply and gave his life to Jesus Christ.

I overheard Curt one night, prostrate on the floor, crying out: "Jesus, You drank the cup for me! You drank the cup for me!" A few months later we sat around a campfire at our camp with students from Florida State University. Curt preached, roaring with passion, pleading with them to catch the revelation of the Lamb and bring it to their generation.

I'm sure you can see why my heart weeps as I watch the Holy Spirit carving a revelation of the Lamb into the hearts of the young. I'm even more overwhelmed as I see them turning and imparting to the next generation.

Never Too Old

Perhaps you think you're too old. I tell my older students at BRSM, "God has brought you here to prepare you as leaders for the next generation." I remind them, "Joshua was eighty when he led the young generation into the Promised Land!" You see, this generation starves for older people who will love them, lead them, mentor them and impart wisdom into their lives.

I heard a story of a seventy-five-year-old blind woman who sat outside a boys' school, with her Bible open. When a student would approach, she would ask him to read an underlined verse for an old blind woman. The young man would read: *"For God so loved the world that he gave his one and only Son, that whoever believes in him shall not perish but have eternal life"* (John 3:16).

Then she would ask, "Do you know what this means?" Almost always the door opened for her to share the Gospel, and she led many young men to the Lord — while seventy-five and blind!

When I was thirteen, I heard a hymn, written by a forty-five-year-old handicapped woman, which changed my life forever. I had tried to find God as long as I can remember, but my parents were unbelievers and I knew nothing about Jesus. A friend had taken me to a revival where I heard the Gospel for the first time in my life. But it wasn't the sermon that drew me; it was the song.

The crowd sang, "Just as I am, without one plea, but that Thy blood was shed for me, and that Thou bidd'st me come to Thee, O Lamb of God, I come! I come!"

I was crying and thinking, "Oh God, I'm too sinful to go up to the altar! I'll go home and pray all day and try to get clean enough to come forward tomorrow and receive Jesus Christ." Then I heard these words: "Just as I am, and waiting not to rid my soul of one dark blot, to Thee whose blood can cleanse each spot, O Lamb of God, I come! I come!"

Suddenly, I understood that the blood of Jesus could cleanse me. I ran forward and prayed to receive Him. I later heard that the woman who wrote "Just As I Am" was filled with disappointment because she was never able to be a missionary.[4] Yet that one song, written by a middle-aged, handicapped woman, has led more people to Jesus Christ than a hundred missionaries. So please, never, never think you're too old!

Lamb-like Humility

If your eyes have been opened to see the Lamb more clearly, I urge you not to feel you've received some "special revelation." There is nothing new about the doctrine of the Lamb. It's as old as the Bible, but it's been cluttered by other teachings which seem more exciting.

We are all expecting a greater wave of glory to flood the Church, but the glory may not come the way you expected. It may slip in quietly and subtly, like Jesus loves to do. He comes through lowly mangers, swaddled in rags of humility, worshiped by poor shepherds. That's why He's using humble worshipers, clothed in Lamb-like meekness, to bring in *the Glory of the Lamb*.

So please keep your heart humble, broken at the foot of the cross. As Judson Cornwall said, in his book *Forbidden*

Glory, "Those who aspire to go higher in God, need to learn to go deeper in humility."[5] He explained, "True humility is not looking down on yourself, but looking up to Christ."[6]

Yes, keep your heart broken at Calvary, joyfully looking up to the Lamb. Like Paul, let your cry be: *"May I never boast except in the cross of our Lord Jesus Christ"* (Galatians 6:14). As humble followers of the Lamb, join the "nameless, faceless ones," the John the Baptist generation, pointing upward to behold the Lamb.

Glory on the Third Day

Hosea prophesied, *"After two days he will revive us; on the third day he will restore us, that we may live in his presence"* (Hosea 6:2). As I write, the third year of the third millennium (since the time of Christ) is ending. I believe the Lord, on this "third day" and in the days to come is breathing from Heaven on a young generation. He is causing them to experience the glory that flows from the Lamb of God.

For this is the day of the glory of God. Jonathan Edwards, considered one of America's finest theologians, looked ahead with visionary perspective and saw a "latter day of glory." He described this as a time "wherein God's people should not only once see the light of God's glory, as Moses, or see it once a year with the high priest, but should dwell and walk continually in it, and it should be their daily light."[7]

We are entering the days when *"the earth will be filled with the knowledge of the glory of the* LORD, *as the waters cover the sea"* (Habakkuk 2:14; see also Isaiah 11:9). It will be the fulfillment of the great Feast of Tabernacles. So great will be this day of glory, it will be as though the Kingdom of Heaven has settled on earth, just as Jesus prayed.

Now at last the fullness of time has come. God is reaching down from Heaven and piercing the veils that have blinded His Church. He's digging through the rubble and causing us to behold His Son as the Lamb.

Even as the last book of the Bible unveiled a revelation of His Son as the Lamb (the book of Revelation), I believe the last move of God will unveil to the Church a revelation of His Son as the Lamb. Then, through the Church, God's Son will be revealed to all the nations of this earth. In seeing the Lamb, we will see more of His resurrection glory, but His glory will cause us to see more of the Lamb.

How else could it be? How could God the Father rip open the veil of His own Son's flesh and allow us to remain so casual about it? How could He pour eternal wrath upon the Darling of His Heart and let us remain oblivious to the depth of such suffering? How could He allow His glory to flood from His pierced One and let us miss it? Impossible!

That's why it's time to bring the Baby out of the water and put Him back in the center of the party. It's time to place God's Masterpiece back over the mantel of the Church. It's time to dig out the debris that covers God's Son as the Lamb and bring the revelation to light. It's time to allow Him to strip the veil from the eyes of His Church and let us behold His Son as the Lamb.

It's my conviction that He will not close this age until His Son is fully revealed as the Lamb. This is not a new revelation. It is simply rediscovering the Gospel.

The Glory of the Gospel

You see, there is divine glory in the Gospel. Paul wrote, *"We possess this precious treasure [the divine Light of the Gospel] in [frail, human] vessels of earth"* (2 Corinthians 4:7, AMP). I believe it is time for the *"divine Light"* of the Gospel to be freshly revealed. And when it is, the resurrection power and glory of the Lamb will flood His Church again.

Paul wrote: *"I want to know Christ and the power of his resurrection and the fellowship of sharing in his sufferings"* (Philippians 3:10). This is not *our* sufferings, but *His* sufferings. It is identifying so deeply with the cup He drank that you can almost feel a drop of the horror He endured.

So let the cross burn deep. Let it consume your soul and scar your heart. For the more you allow the cross to brand your heart, the more resurrection glory will explode from your wound.

It's like placing a lighted match to oil. When fire touches oil, combustion occurs. In a far greater way, when the fire of the cup touches the fuel of the Spirit, the resurrection glory will burst into flames in your heart. Then, ultimately, we will see the full conflagration of glory which God wants to bring through His Church to all the nations of this earth.

Leaving John

The sun has begun to set beyond the sea, leaving only a hazy pink glow on the horizon. The old apostle lays his head back against the rocks.

Even as he pens the words to the book that will conclude the canon of Scripture, he realizes that the whole Bible points to the Lamb. The Old Testament shows God's preparation for His coming Son, the blood of lambs splashing every page. He gilds every page of the New Testament with resurrection glory, pouring from the exalted Lamb.

John is exhausted from seeing this vision, but he's only just begun. In the days to follow, the Lord will open Heaven to him many times and he will see his beloved Lamb. We will pick up this story in several sequels to this book.[8]

"May the Lamb Receive His Due Reward!"

Now, as you close these covers, I want to leave you with one final thought. A young nobleman wandered into a cathedral in Europe to admire the architecture. Suddenly, he caught a glimpse of a powerful painting of the crucifixion. It struck him in the heart. He stood and gazed at it for hours.

He saw the blood dripping from every wound. He saw love glowing in every tear. He saw grace shining in every brushstroke. The artist had been saved by Jesus from a life of deep darkness and sin. Now he painted mercy in every line, forgiveness in every blood drop. The picture was compelling and it gripped the young man's heart. Then he read the caption beneath the painting: "I did this for thee; what wilt thou do for Me?"

The young man fell to his knees, sobbing. With all his heart he promised God that for the rest of his life he would glorify the Lamb for what He suffered on the cross.

You, too, have stood at the feet of the Crucified One and looked up at the Lamb of God. You've seen the love distilled in every tear, the mercy in His blood drops, the glory shining in His eyes. Won't you live to tell others about *the Glory of the Lamb*?

The young man in the story above was Count Nikolaus Ludwig von Zinzendorf. He went on to found the Moravians. Because of Zinzendorf's encounter with the Lamb, the watchword of the Moravians was this: "May the Lamb receive His due reward for what He suffered on the cross!"

Won't you make this the cry of your heart as well? Won't you spend the rest of your life bringing glory to the Lamb for what He did for you? Above all, won't you live to give Jesus the reward of His suffering?

What is that reward? It's people. It's souls for the Lamb. Won't you go out now and bring Him the reward He so richly deserves?

If you will, you'll be amazed at what awaits you. For when your life is over, you will look into the shining face of Jesus. You will see the tears of pleasure shimmering in His eyes, and you will hear Him say, *"Well done!"* Then you will know, through the fruits of your life on earth — Jesus has received the glory He deserves for giving Himself as your Lamb!

Endnotes

1. Peter, James and Paul had all been martyred by now. Tradition holds that they tried to boil John in oil, but he wouldn't die, so he was exiled to this Island of Patmos where God gave him the Revelation.
2. John R. W. Stott, *The Cross of Christ* (Downers Grove, IL: Inter-Varsity Press, 1986), p. 343.
3. This video was produced by Leesia Mason, Melissa Clegg, Cheryl Logan and Rebecca Luskey.
4. Charlotte Elliott, "Just As I Am."
5. Judson Cornwall, *Forbidden Glory: Portraits of Pride* (Hagerstown, MD: McDougal Publishing, 2001), p. 225.
6. Ibid., p. 228.
7. Jonathan Edwards, "An Humble Attempt to Promote Explicit Agreement and Visible Union of God's People, in Extraordinary Prayer for the Revival of Religion and the Advancement of Christ's Kingdom on Earth," *The Works of Jonathan Edwards,* Vol. 2 (Edinburgh: Banner of Truth Trust), p. 287.
8. Meanwhile, I urge you to get my book *A Revelation of the Lamb for America* (McDougal Publishing, 2002). The Lord is using it to help people in this country see the Lamb. If your heart has been moved and you want to help spread the message of the Lamb, please get this book and pass it on. In a small way, it will help give Jesus the glory He deserves for giving His life as the Lamb. The first of the three future books will be *The Cry of a Generation,* which will show how God's Lamb answers the cry of a fatherless, young generation. This one to the youth will not be presented through John's eyes because I want it to speak directly to the wounds and needs of the teenagers. However, the two books following that one will be sequels to this book. The first to be published will be *A Revelation of the Lamb for Israel,* which shows how to bring a revelation of the Lamb to Jewish people and will give God's answer to the Holocaust. The final book in this series will be entitled *A Revelation of the Lamb for the Nations.* It will be filled with stories of young men and women who are carrying a revelation of the Lamb to the nations of this world. I can hardly wait to tell their stories!